HELPING STUDENTS FIX

PROBLEMS

and Avoid Crises

HELPING STUDENTS FIX PROBLEMS

and Avoid Crises

An Easy-to-Use
Intervention Resource
for Grades 1-4

Lawrence J. Greene

CORWIN PRESS
A SAGE Publications Company
Thousand Oaks, California

Copyright © 2005 by Corwin Press

All rights reserved. When forms and sample documents are included, their use is authorized only by educators, local school sites, and/or noncommercial or nonprofit entities who have purchased the book. Except for that usage, no part of this book may be reproduced or utilized in any form or by any means, electronic or mechanical, including photocopying, recording, or by any information storage and retrieval system, without permission in writing from the publisher.

For information:

Corwin Press
A Sage Publications Company
2455 Teller Road
Thousand Oaks, California 91320
www.corwinpress.com

Sage Publications Ltd.
1 Oliver's Yard
55 City Road
London EC1Y 1SP
United Kingdom

Sage Publications India Pvt. Ltd.
B-42, Panchsheel Enclave
Post Box 4109
New Delhi 110 017 India

Printed in the United States of America.

Library of Congress Cataloging-in-Publication Data

Greene, Lawrence J.
Helping students fix problems and avoid crises:
An easy-to-use intervention resource for grades 1–4 / Lawrence J. Greene.
       p. cm.
Includes index.
ISBN 1–4129–0469–2 (cloth)—ISBN 1–4129–0470–6 (pbk.)
   1. Socialization. 2. Life skills—Study and teaching (Elementary)
3. Problem solving—Study and teaching (Elementary) I. Title.
LC192.4.G75 2005
302'.07—dc22   2004029804

This book is printed on acid-free paper.

05   06   07   08   09   10   9   8   7   6   5   4   3   2   1

Acquisitions Editor:	Faye Zucker
Editorial Assistant:	Gem Rabanera
Production Editor:	Laureen A. Shea
Copy Editor:	Elizabeth S. Budd
Typesetter:	C&M Digitals (P) Ltd.
Proofreader:	Libby Larson
Indexer:	Pamela Van Huss
Cover Designer:	Rose Storey

Contents

Introduction

A first grader wanders alone on the playground during recess. No one acknowledges him. No one asks him to play.

Second-grade girls tease a classmate because she is overweight, and the boys call her names. She responds by eating more food.

A child winces from embarrassment when she's called on to read aloud in class. She stumbles over virtually every word, and, despite the stern, admonishing glare of the teacher, the other children giggle as she struggles to decipher the letters and sounds.

A third grader is considered weird by his classmates because he can't pay attention or sit still. He impulsively blurts out inappropriate comments without raising his hand, wanders aimlessly around the room, and continually disrupts the class. Seemingly oblivious to the continual reproaches he receives from his teacher, he chronically misbehaves and, in so doing, further alienates his classmates.

An uncoordinated child is invariably picked last when sides are chosen during PE. The other children moan when he ends up on their team. Each time he misjudges a fly ball or strikes out, his teammates laugh and groan.

All children experience problems from time to time. These dilemmas go with the territory of being a child and are part of the developmental learning curve. In the long run, the vast majority of the predicaments prove inconsequential, and most children cannot even remember the previous day's dilemma. Having an argument with a friend, being kept in the classroom during recess for misbehavior, or getting a poor grade on a homework assignment are unlikely to leave a permanent imprint on a child's psyche, unless, of course, the scenarios are recurring and scripted.

Of far greater concern are the more intractable problems that are often directly attributable to the student's attitudes and behavior. Children who chronically lie, tease, steal, bully, cheat, spread rumors, or act in socially inappropriate ways are transmitting a clear message that they are unhappy campers. Their actions are certain to generate undesirable repercussions that typically include peer rejection, alienation, and repeated admonitions and punishments from teachers and parents.

Youngsters who are socially rejected, bullied, belittled, teased for looking or acting different, disparaged for having learning problems or other disabilities, or scorned for poor athletic skills are clearly at psychological risk. Their traumatic experiences in the classroom and on the playground are all but certain to profoundly, and perhaps indelibly, warp their perceptions about themselves and their world.

Maladjustment and inappropriate behavior that trigger derision and estrangement should not be dismissed as run-of-the-mill conditions that children should be able to simply shrug off. Yellow and red flags are flapping in the wind. These yellow flags quickly become red flags when teasing, bullying, lying, or stealing is added to the mix.

Children wrestling with seemingly intractable problems and those on the receiving end of unkind behavior—even if the reactions of their classmates are attributable to the rejected child's own seemingly intentional maladaptive conduct—require adult assistance in coming to grips with the underlying issues and in resolving the dilemmas. If this help isn't provided, aggrieved children may conclude that the predicaments are insoluble and that the crises are unavoidable. Feelings of frustration and futility can easily overwhelm belea-guered youngsters who lack the requisite analytical thinking skills, problem-solving capabilities, and insight to resolve their problems.

Social estrangement and social deprecation can shake the very foundation of a young child's self-concept. Unless alienated children are furnished with effective problem-solving tools, they are at risk for developing a host of defense and compensatory mechanisms that will magnify and exacerbate the situation. These self-protecting mechanisms may range from oppositional behavior and conduct disorders at one end of the spectrum to depression and self-destructive, or even suicidal, tendencies at the other end.

In theory, our society, and especially our schools, should have learned this immutable lesson about the implications of social estrangement from the events at Columbine High School in Littleton, Colorado. Certainly, this tragedy was extreme, but we continue to be confronted with the harmful effects of maladjustment as other troubled students in schools across the nation express their unhappiness, social alienation, and despair through acts of violent behavior. Sobering as this violence is, we must remind ourselves that for every child who expresses anguish through explosive and violent rage, there are thousands of others who suffer in silence. Their self-esteem is demolished, and their frustration and anger implode and trigger despondency, demoralization, and depression. These children may attempt to hide their unhappiness with contrived conduct that is unconsciously designed to either defect or draw attention, but their despair is palpable if one looks beneath surface appearances. Class clowns, bullies, braggarts, instigators, and rumor spreaders are simply compensating for their own feelings of inadequacy.

BEING ATTUNED

Aware teachers, counselors, and school administrators clearly recognize the potential risks that children face when confronted with seemingly intractable life dilemmas. The natural impulse of many of these educators is to intervene proactively. Their concerns typically include the following:

- How can I help my students deal with the problems they're facing?
- How can I help my students develop a better understanding of the issues?
- How can I make my students aware of their role in creating the problem?

- How can I provide appropriate guidance and support?
- How can I intervene without sending the message that I will take ownership of every problem that my students encounter?
- How can I discourage maladaptive behavior and encourage adaptive and socially acceptable behavior?
- How can I be sure that I'm doing everything to help emotionally at-risk children deal with troubling situations?
- How can I sensitize my students to the feelings of their classmates, and how can I help them appreciate the pain they are inflicting by teasing, isolating, disparaging, or bullying other children?

CAN I REALLY DO IT?

Right now, you may be thinking, "I'm not a clinical psychologist, and I haven't been trained to deal with these issues." If you are indeed thinking these thoughts, you're absolutely right. No, you are not a clinical psychologist, and no, you haven't been trained to deal with your students' psychological problems. This having been said, it's equally important to assert your assets and talents. You are a professional educator. You understand how kids tick, and you have a broad range of skills. With an effective instruction model, you're certainly capable of teaching your students how to fix many of the common everyday problems and handle many of the common everyday crises that they face. Teaching children how to resolve the pain-producing dilemmas they face in life is actually not as challenging as you might believe. There's an added payoff: Teaching your students these problem-solving skills can also be exceptionally rewarding.

Of course, when children manifest significant social maladjustment and inappropriate conduct, this behavior may indicate significant underlying psychological issues that require immediate intervention by a competent mental health professional. Troubled students should be referred as soon as possible to the school psychologist or school counselor. (*Please note:* In the Appendices you'll find an inventory of red-flag behaviors that are generally symptomatic of psychological problems and a second inventory of red-flag behaviors that are generally symptomatic of psychological overlay. The appropriate school personnel should be alerted when you observe children exhibiting these behaviors.)

This book is not intended to transform you into a clinical psychologist. Rather, it's designed to provide you with a practical and easy-to-use blueprint for helping your students acquire more effective analytical thinking, decision-making, and problem-solving skills. The program also shows you how to help students in Grades 1–4 acquire greater compassion, values, ethics, empathy, and emotional resiliency.

The strategies in this book are based on a core principle, namely, that educators, counselors, and school administrators have a compelling responsibility to furnish students with a range of functional life skills. This obligation is a societal constant that transcends time and culture. Whether the objectives in a developing country are to teach children how to use a sewing machine, repair an engine, or avoid landmines, or the objectives in a developed country are to teach children how to do research for a term paper, use a computer, or deal with teasing, the instructional pedagogy is essentially the same. You teach the relevant steps and procedures systematically. You show children how to break tasks and challenges down into manageable pieces (the "divide and conquer" principle). You model. You structure opportunities for practice. You provide feedback. You affirm progress. You provide help, support, and encouragement.

Sound familiar? Of course it does. You apply these very same instructional principles every day! As a teacher, you already know how to instruct, guide, and mentor children. But perhaps you didn't realize that you could use the same basic, commonsense procedures when teaching students how to handle problems and avoid crises. The premise is simple: Children should be taught how to identify and resolve problems *before* they become monumental, debilitating, and seemingly insoluble dilemmas.

HOW THE PROGRAM WORKS

Each unit in *Helping Students Fix Problems and Avoid Crises* focuses on a specific topic that could trigger pain in a child's life. The format is simple and consistent. The key issues are succinctly examined in the educator-directed section at the beginning of the unit. The unit then segues to a short child-directed, read-aloud story that presents the issues in terms that students aged six through nine years can easily grasp and assimilate. The evocative and engaging stories require approximately five to ten minutes to read aloud. Teachers may elect to have students read the anecdotes, or they may prefer to read the stories to the class. The questions that follow each story are designed to elicit reactions, stimulate critical and strategic thinking, enhance sensitivity and compassion, improve problem-solving capabilities, and develop verbal communication skills. Optional pencil-and-paper activities and reproducible exercises are provided to reinforce understanding and assimilation of the issues and ensure mastery of the skills being taught. The overriding goal of each unit is to convince students that with guidance and sufficient practice, they can successfully handle many of the seemingly insoluble problems that they're facing.

Children do not need to be struggling with the particular problem addressed in a unit to derive benefit from the analytical process. For example, youngsters who have no difficulty making friends can certainly profit from a better understanding of how their unpopular classmates feel, and children who learn effortlessly can also profit from a better appreciation and understanding of the frustration and embarrassment that children with learning problems often experience. These insights are requisites to their acquiring enhanced empathy.

The modeled interactive teaching methods incorporate *cognitive behavioral change procedures*. These procedures emphasize

- *Relevancy*—the skills being taught directly relate to real-world issues.
- *Insight*—heightened awareness of the underlying factors helps children better handle problems and crises.
- *Instruction*—easy-to-use and easy-to-understand procedures enhance mastery.
- *Reinforcement*—repeated opportunities to practice ensure assimilation.

- ***Behavioral Change***—deliberately orchestrated successes encourage the use of newly learned skills.
- ***Application***—recurrent use of newly learned skills embeds productive habits.

By design, the material in this program can be seamlessly woven into any academic curriculum or counseling program. You may, for example, decide to devote one or two twenty-five minute blocks of time each week to reading and discussing a selected story.

You are about to add a critically important dimension to your interaction with your students. You are about to become a powerful *life skills mentor.* You'll discover that the process of showing children how to resolve problems and handle crises is not only doable, it's also enjoyable and immensely satisfying. Of course, as a professional educator, counselor, or administrator, you're already serving as a mentor in a wide range of venues. This program will furnish additional tools and expand your reach and influence into areas that might otherwise be overlooked or deliberately avoided.

Imagine the sense of relief children experience when they discover that the problems that are causing them anguish can actually be fixed. Then imagine being the person who guides children to this potentially life-altering discovery. Isn't this one of the most prized payoffs for the professional educator?

The modern educator cannot content himself or herself with exclusively teaching academic skills and course content. Children in the world of the twenty-first century are facing too many problems, challenges, temptations, and crises to be left to their own devices. Many are foundering because they are ill prepared to handle these trials, and they desperately need our guidance so that they can develop strategies for understanding and sorting out the issues and handling the dilemmas that might otherwise overwhelm them. You have the opportunity to serve as one of their primary guides and to help lead them safely through the minefield.

Let's get started.

ACKNOWLEDGMENTS

Corwin Press and the author extend their thanks to the following reviewers for their contributions to this volume:

Robert DiGiulio
Education Professor
Johnson State College
Johnson, Vermont

Kevin Fall
Associate Professor and Chair
Department of Education
    and Counseling
Loyola University New Orleans
New Orleans, Louisiana

Mary Ann Sweet
Counselor
Tomball Elementary School
Tomball, Texas

Beverly Eidmann
Principal
Manzanita Elementary School
Newbury Park, California

About the Author

Lawrence J. Greene, a graduate of the Stanford University Graduate School of Education, is a nationally recognized author, educational therapist, consultant, and curriculum developer who has worked with more than ten thousand struggling students during a clinical career spanning thirty years. He has written eighteen books, and he has trained thousands of teachers in graduate programs at the university level. His educational curricula are currently used in elementary schools, middle schools, high schools, colleges, and universities throughout the world, and his books have been translated into languages ranging from Chinese to Spanish.

Other Books by Lawrence J. Greene

Kids Who Hate School

Kids Who Underachieve

Learning Disabilities and Your Child

Getting Smarter

Think Smart, Study Smart

Smarter Kids

Teachers' Desk Reference Guide to Learning Problems

Improving Your Child's Schoolwork

The Life-Smart Kid

Finding Help When Your Child Is Struggling in School

Roadblocks to Learning

Winning the Study Game

Study Wise

Study Max: Improving Study Skills in Grades 9–12

The Resistant Learner

Strategies for Success (forthcoming)

For my son, Joshua Ryan Greene

*Your spirit and zest still enthrall me. I shall always
be thankful for the joy you have brought into my life.*

Unit 1

The Child Who Doesn't Have Friends

For Educators

Examining the Dynamics and
Implications of Social Rejection

Human beings are more akin to lions than to tigers. Tigers are solitary animals. They hunt alone and, after mating, the female leaves the male. She stays with her cubs only until they are able to hunt on their own, and then she abandons them.

Lions, on the other hand, are social animals. They live in prides, hunt together, function as a unit, and find security in their social order, roles, and interaction.

Children are also social animals. During the early formative years, their parents satisfy virtually all of their needs for human interaction, but when they enter preschool, they begin to crave companionship with their peers. They delight in interactive play and in sharing discoveries about their world with their friends. Through this interplay, they acquire socialization skills and assimilate the rules for acceptable and unacceptable conduct. They learn that some behaviors foster friendships, and other behaviors deter friendships. They discover that there are social consequences for their actions, and they realize that mutually shared interests and pleasures bind them to other like-minded children. With guidance from their preschool teachers and parents, they absorb lessons about sharing, decorum, and resolving conflicts. By means of trial and error, they ideally identify, either consciously or unconsciously, the behaviors and attitudes that have the potential to make them popular or unpopular with their peers.

For hard-to-explain reasons, certain children never assimilate these critically important social lessons. In some cases, their off-putting behavior may be attributable to inherited temperament or to distinctive personality traits and aptitudes. Although these children hunger for acceptance, companionship, and popularity, they haven't a clue about how to make and maintain friendships. Feeling isolated and rejected, they hover on the social periphery. Other children rarely, if ever, invite them to play. They have no special friends with whom they can share discoveries, experiences, and pleasures. By the age

Author's Note: The male and female genders will be used variously in different units.

of six or seven, they are already keenly aware of the pain associated with social estrangement. And worse, the maladaptive patterns they establish in first grade may persist throughout their life with potentially disastrous psychological consequences.

STRUGGLING WITH SEEMINGLY INSOLUBLE PROBLEMS

Social rejection cuts to the core of a child's self-esteem. Having no one to play with cannot help but trigger feelings of isolation and alienation. On either a conscious or unconscious level, the rejected child feels intrinsically flawed. He may attempt to compensate for his social difficulties by retreating into a fantasy world or by latching onto activities that provide a surrogate for having friends. The activities may include watching TV, reading, playing video games, or resorting to parallel play (e.g., bouncing a ball or using the monkey bars while surrounded by other children who are playing together, but not interacting with these children). Despite these efforts to compensate, the socially isolated child is destined to suffer terribly. Classmates do not invite him to birthday parties. They don't call him on the telephone. They don't want to sit next to him on the school bus. They don't initiate playdates. Rejected children soon begin to feel invisible. They have no one with whom to share the excitement, wo ders, joys, and discoveries of childhood, and the pain they experience can be excruciating.

Lacking insight and perspective, most young children cannot identify what's causing them to be rejected, even though the causal factors may be readily apparent to an adult observer. The socially alienated child may be overly aggressive or overly shy. He may continually misbehave or get other children in trouble. He may be a bully or the class clown. He may be terribly spoiled, self-centered, or immature. He may be physically uncoordinated and do poorly in sports. He may act in unconventional ways. He may have attention deficit/ hyperactivity disorder (ADHD) and be disruptive in class and on the playground. He may have learning problems that cause him to struggle in school. He may wear clothing that doesn't conform to the accepted mode. He may look different physically, have a nature that's considered too gentle or timid, have interests that are perceived as weird, or be excessively self-conscious and unable to interact comfortably with other children. In some cases, the socially estranged child may be highly intelligent or talented in a particular area and may not be able to relate to other, less gifted children. Whatever the reasons for the child's inability to relate successfully to his peers, the effect of the estrangement can be emotionally devastating.

When teasing compounds peer rejection, the potential for children to become dispirited and depressed increases significantly. Unless the problems are addressed and a proactive plan is put in place to resolve the dilemma, these children are at great emotional risk.

Ostracized and disparaged children are not the only ones who suffer. Their parents and teachers share their pain. Seeing a child being hurt is heartrending, and the natural adult instinct is to intervene to offer protection. Unfortunately, the well-meaning efforts of concerned parents and teachers often prove ineffectual, and the problems persist and continue to exact their emotional toll. To their dismay, parents and teachers usually discover that they can't take ownership of children's problems, nor can they shield children from social rejection. The best they can do is provide support, assistance, and guidance. In the final analysis, the most potent form of adult intervention is to help children develop functional strategies for identifying and resolving their own problems.

THE NUTS AND BOLTS OF SELF-ESTEEM

The foundation for self-esteem is formed during the early formative years of life, and a child's evolving self-concept is profoundly influenced by his life experiences. Children who feel loved and secure, experience success in the classroom and on the playground, receive positive feedback at home and in school, and form and maintain friendships are far more likely to feel good about themselves than those who do not experience these critically important affirmations. Children who possess a positive self-image typically project self-confidence, display socially acceptable and age-appropriate behavior, develop independence, capitalize on their natural abilities, and have little difficulty interacting successfully with their peers.

Conversely, children who don't feel good about themselves usually act congruently with their diminished self-concept. They tend to act inappropriately and maladaptively, and their behavior is almost invariably off-putting to the very children whose acceptance they crave. A cycle is thus created: Reduced self-esteem triggers maladaptive conduct that, in turn, triggers social rejection, alienation, and isolation. This estrangement further damages the already tenuous self-concept of the socially inept child. The self-defeating dynamic can produce dire psychological consequences not only during childhood, but also down the road when alienated and socially challenged children become adults.

Certainly, a child's self-concept can be enhanced after the early formative years of preschool and kindergarten, and the self-confidence and social skills of the child who has gotten off to a shaky start can be significantly improved with effective adult intervention and support. Positive life experiences that are carefully orchestrated by teachers in the lower grades of elementary school can play an instrumental role in inducing this growth.

Effective adult intervention, however, does not translate into adults' taking ownership of children's social problems. The far more effectual intercession is for teachers and parents to help socially inept children develop practical and functional problem-solving strategies and to provide them with the tools they require to understand the issues and deal with their relationship dilemmas. By methodically teaching at-risk students how to handle the problems and by engineering personal victories for these youngsters, adults are, in effect, creating important opportunities for children to begin feeling better about themselves. The resulting feelings of "OK-ness" will almost invariably translate into enhanced social interaction.

IDENTIFYING AND EXPRESSING FEELINGS

Educators know full well that their students' responses to stimuli are frequently driven by emotions that are bubbling just below the surface. A situation, rebuke, reprimand, rejection, or frustration can stoke the fire and cause the cauldron to boil. Suddenly, the feelings erupt, and a child may lash out or begin crying inconsolably.

Children sometimes express their emotions openly, and sometimes they warehouse their emotions. The expressed or repressed feelings can be overpowering and can trigger confusion, anxiety, fear, and despair. To avoid feeling helpless, children often acquire a range of coping and defense mechanisms that may be functional in the short term but are likely to be psychologically damaging in the long term. The potpourri of unconscious ego-protecting devices to which socially at-risk children often unconsciously resort—denial, rationalizations, and delusions—allows youngsters to avoid having to confront the factors that are causing their social estrangement. Despite their best efforts, the avoided feelings will not go away, and these deflected negative emotions cannot help but distort socially estranged children's perceptions about themselves and the world.

No attuned educator would dispute that not having friends can be a devastating experience for children. To prevent self-concept damage, unpopular children must be helped to realize that predicaments such as rejection and loneliness can be resolved if they identify what's causing their social difficulties, think creatively, and brainstorm practical solutions to the problem. By encouraging students to examine the dynamics of successful versus unsuccessful social interaction and by creating a safe context for them to do so, you can play an instrumental role in helping alienated students identify what they can do proactively to make themselves more acceptable to their peers.

The realization that problems are fixable and crises are solvable can lift a heavy burden from the shoulders of dispirited children. Conversely, youngsters who conclude that their social situation is hopeless are clearly at risk emotionally. There are two likely outcomes: Their frustration and demoralization may *implode* and cause them to become depressed, self-sabotaging, and dysfunctional, or their frustration and demoralization may *explode* and trigger emotional outbursts, acting-out behavior, and aggression.

That young children often try to stuff down emotions that are painful and confusing is understandable. To insulate themselves from having to confront unpleasant feelings, they may deny that they're in pain and make up stories to reduce their discomfort, deflect attention, and hide their sadness and vulnerability. They may pretend that they have friends when they have none, or they may retreat into a fantasy world populated by imaginary companions. When parents and school personnel attempt to elicit information about what's going on, they often hit a brick wall. The common and barely audible "I don't know" response to their queries can effectively shut down meaningful communication. This response is clearly a defense mechanism, but it may also indicate that these uncommunicative children cannot identify their problem or cannot find the words to express their distress.

CONCEPT AND APPLICATION

Examining another child's dilemmas and feelings of alienation can be a highly effective technique for eliciting responses, stimulating class discussions, expanding awareness, and honing analytical skills. It is generally far less threatening for children, and particularly for those who are in crisis, to explore another child's predicament than it is for them to plunge directly into the emotional maelstrom and explore their own dilemmas.

The story that follows is specifically designed to encourage students to look at the issue of making friends and to express their feelings and thoughts. Justin, the protagonist, functions as an emotional surrogate for children who are struggling with social problems. The alienated students in your class are likely to find it less daunting to discuss Justin's plight than to talk about their own personal experiences with rejection.

As you examine the story and pose questions, you want to be patient and supportive. Highly defended children should not be pressured into sharing their feelings in front of their classmates. Some may prefer to listen rather than actively participate. This does not mean that these more reticent children are not profiting from examining the story or that they are not acquiring important insights about themselves and their social modus operandi. At an opportune moment, a simple statement such as, "It sure can make you sad when you have no one to play with," or a simple question such as, "Has anyone in this class ever felt lonely?" could open the floodgates and could lead to an exchange of ideas about friendship.

DEVELOPING ANALYTICAL THINKING SKILLS

Most young children are preoccupied with their own immediate issues and concerns. They're hungry, happy, or sad, and the world revolves around their personal needs and desires. There's nothing intrinsically wrong with this self-preoccupation. It reflects developmentally age-appropriate behavior. The conduct becomes problematic only when children are so self-absorbed that they fail to recognize that they are being insensitive to the feelings of others and are wittingly or unwittingly causing pain.

Few children give conscious thought to why they reject or make fun of another child. Their reactions are essentially visceral. They observe that another child is in some way different, be it his clothes, his behavior, or his responses. They may see the child acting inappropriately and may exclude him from their social group because they cannot easily relate to his behavior. In most situations, children react without even being consciously aware of their selection and rejection criteria. They may simply conclude, "He's weird."

Teaching students to consider the reasons for their decisions and judgments and training them to assess the justness of their behavior is integral to developing their analytical thinking capabilities. This instruction not only plays a crucial role in helping children develop and strengthen their analytical and critical thinking skills, it also plays an equally crucial role in helping them develop character, empathy, and compassion for classmates who may not fit into the cookie mold. The goal is for students to become more aware of the selection criteria they use when accepting and rejecting other children. The ancillary goal is for students to be more tolerant of children who act and think differently.

By helping students understand the dynamics of their own problems and those their classmates face, you're providing them with a powerful problem-solving resource. Insight can help a bully understand a fundamental cause-and-effect principle—namely, that other children don't like him because he's aggressive, hostile, and controlling. This insight can also help the bully realize that by altering his behavior, he can achieve social acceptance. So, too, can guided insight help the child who lies, steals, or breaks the rules when playing a game realize that other children don't want to interact with him because of his selfish behavior. This realization clearly suggests obvious solutions to the social problems that are directly linked to his behavior.

Helping socially inept children acquire greater insight into their maladaptive and off-putting behavior does not necessarily require the intervention of a mental health professional, although certainly there are unhappy and chronically self-sabotaging children who should be professionally evaluated. In many instances, however, an insightful and sensitive classroom teacher equipped with an effective instructional program can lead students to a better understanding of their role in causing their own social estrangement and can help these children realize that alternative behaviors and attitudes can foster greater acceptance. The teacher can also help other students become more accepting of classmates who are perceived as undesirable.

Young children are not introspective by nature. Living primarily in the here and now (except, of course, when they're looking forward to a special event such as a birthday or a trip to Disneyland), they are seldom motivated to explore the underlying issues that impel their feelings, thoughts, and actions. This obliviousness is perfectly normal, because young children are primarily reactive to stimuli at this stage of their development. A particular situation may elicit an emotional response that could range from joy and satisfaction at one end of the continuum to pain and fear at the other. The responses are usually automatic and typically short-circuit logic and reason. Despite this natural proclivity, some situations require thought, and given the young child's natural resistance to reflection, creative strategies are required to elicit this behavior.

OBJECTIVES FOR
ENHANCING STUDENTS' AWARENESS

- Sharpening students' observational skills (e.g., "He's feeling sad because no one plays with him.")
- Stimulating students to be more introspective and insightful (e.g., "I've been mean to him.")

- Training students to look beyond surface appearance (e.g., "Maybe he doesn't like sports because he isn't good at them.")
- Teaching students to think analytically and critically (e.g., "It's OK for kids not to like the same things and not to dress the same way.")
- Helping students acquire more effective problem-solving skills (e.g., "I know he likes chess, and maybe I could ask him to play chess with me.")
- Encouraging students to become more compassionate (e.g., "I bet it would make him happy if I treated him more nicely.")

The story and the questions, guided discussions, interactive activities, and reproducible paper-and-pencil exercises provide an ideal context for attaining these objectives.

CAN CHILDREN BE TAUGHT TO BE MORE EMPATHETIC?

The answer to this question is unequivocally *yes!* And the ideal time to launch the enhanced empathy instructional process is when students are in Grades 1–4. Just as prejudice and intolerance can be taught, so, too, can empathy and compassion for others be taught.

In many situations, children's spontaneous visceral responses can be endearing. The child who gets a hit in a baseball game, sinks a basket, wins a spelling bee, receives an invitation to a classmate's party, or climbs a tortuous trail to the top of a steep hill is likely to express unfettered joy. Conversely, the child who strikes out, answers a question incorrectly in class, is reprimanded by his teacher for misbehavior, or gets a poor grade on a test is likely to feel immediate, albeit temporary, sadness. These spontaneous responses, however, can be problematic when children fail to recognize the negative impact that certain attitudes and behaviors have on their peers. This lack of awareness, sensitivity, and empathy is reflected in the acts of unkindness and selfishness that young children sometimes demonstrate when interacting with other children.

The more attuned children become to other children's feelings and the more aware they become of the impact that their actions have on others, the less likely they are to be unkind and selfish. You want your students to appreciate why having friends is important not only to them, but to other children as well. You want to sensitize them to the sadness that other students experience when they're rejected or disparaged. You want to teach them to appreciate and respect diversity, be it cultural, religious, racial, or behavioral. You want to encourage them to consider the reasons for their preferences, attitudes, and behavior. You want them to realize that children need not look the same, dress the same, or act the same to be accepted and appreciated. This is the essence of empathy, and empathy is one of the legs on which character development rests.

Children who acquire heightened compassion for others are capable of wondrously kind and caring deeds. These deeds will benefit not only the recipients, they will also make the children performing the deeds feel good about themselves. Certainly, every educator wants to help children recognize that being nice to others can produce immense gratification. These more compassionate children will grow up to be more compassionate adults who will someday ideally raise their own kind and caring children. Teaching children to be kind and considerate of others is eminently doable.

EXAMINING THE STORY

The description of the social problems of the child highlighted in the student-directed anecdote will undoubtedly resonate in children who identify with him. These children have firsthand experience with the pain of being excluded and of feeling estranged and lonely. (*Please note:* At this point, you may find it beneficial to skip ahead and read the story on page 15 so that the following examination of the issues is more concrete.)

Justin's story describes a socially rejected child's sadness, but, at the same time, it also delivers a positive message, namely, that unpopular children can take practical steps to make friends. Imagine the relief that an alienated child will experience when he discovers that he's not forever fated to be a social outcast. By actively involving your students in the process of figuring out how to help Justin solve his problem, you affirm that it's possible for them to devise practical and creative solutions to their *own* problems. The mind-set becomes: "If he can do it, I can do it, too."

Justin's story, of course, isn't directed exclusively at children with social problems. It's also aimed at socially adept youngsters who are oblivious to the sadness that unpopular children experience every day. Sensitizing students who take their popularity for granted and exposing them to the feelings of children who struggle to establish friendships can be an invaluable eye-opener. Ideally, this exposure will help them become more aware and caring.

THE QUESTIONS THAT FOLLOW THE STORY

After reading the anecdote in the student content, you will find a series of questions that highlight and probe the key issues that are raised. You certainly don't need to pose all the questions, and you want to avoid giving children the impression that they're being interrogated. You also want to recognize that the responses of a third grader are likely to be more perceptive and insightful than those of a first grader. The questions are intended to be a catalyst for discussion. You may ultimately decide to examine only a few of the issues broached in the story. This is perfectly OK, especially in the case of younger children.

It's important to acknowledge and affirm your students' expressed reactions, feelings, ideas, and insights, even if they appear off target. When you conclude that children are not "getting it," you might redirect their thinking by suggesting another way of looking at the issue. For example, you might say, "What do you think about this idea?"

You want your students to feel that you're interested in and appreciate what they're saying. Comments that clearly communicate this and that stimulate thinking and discussion include the following:

- "That's very interesting."
- "Can you tell me more about that?"
- "That's a very good point."
- "What caused you to conclude that?"
- "Let me see if I understand what you are saying. . . ."
- "Does anyone have a different idea about this?"

CAUSE-AND-EFFECT PRINCIPLES

Children who function *at cause* and confront their problems have a significant advantage over those who function *at effect* and become resigned and beaten down by their problems. The former recognize that they can take deliberate steps to handle challenges and predicaments. The latter see themselves as victims who have no recourse but to accept their fate passively. With guidance and sufficient opportunities to practice analytical thinking and problem solving, students can learn how to make proactive *at cause* responses to problems a habit.

Encouraging children to assess and weigh the pros and cons of their choices and behavior and training them to consider cause-and-effect principles when responding to events in their life is instrumental in stimulating the development of critical thinking skills. Four core questions are integral with the analytical thinking modus operandi that you want to instill:

- What am I doing?
- Why am I doing it?
- What are the potential consequences?
- Should I reconsider what I'm doing?

Yes, it's true that young children are self-absorbed and are not introspective by nature at this stage in their development, and, yes, children do not need to pose these questions in all situations. At the same time, it's also true that systematically teaching students to think more analytically and critically is an essential component in the process of preparing them to handle life's challenges successfully. Children who are trained to consider the pluses and minuses of their options and the possible consequences *before* they act are far less likely to respond mindlessly and make seriously flawed choices.

BRAINSTORMING

Children require accessible hands-on tools if they are to extricate themselves from their problems. The following *brainstorming tree* (Figure 1.1) provides children with a template for visually conceptualizing problems and devising possible solutions. The template can be superimposed on virtually any problem and will make the problem-solving procedure more concrete. You'll probably want to make multiple photocopies of the graphic. Children who are visual learners should especially appreciate this easy-to-use problem-solving template.

Figure 1.1   Brainstorming Tree for Solving Problems (Blank)

Brainstormed Solution

As you can see in Figure 1.2, the problem in this unit is succinctly described on the line above the tree, and brainstormed solutions are inserted in the circles at the end of each branch on the tree. You'll note that one of the solutions is inserted on the line that appears below the tree. This is the solution that the student or students believe is best. Ideally, the selected solution will be reasonable and practical.

In subsequent units, you can have students use this brainstorming template to define the problem highlighted in the story. After the class discussion and after students have completed the activities, they could insert additional brainstormed solutions to the highlighted problem that were not actually examined in the story. They would then select what they believe are the most effective of these solutions and write them on the line below the tree. This procedure could be completed individually, as a class activity, for homework, or in small cooperative learning groups.

You'll need to model how to use the brainstorming tree, and you'll need to model how to define the problem accurately and concisely. This can be tricky for students, but once they get the hang of it, the brainstorming procedure should become easier and ideally increasingly automatic. The message you want to communicate clearly to your students is that problems can be solved if we identify them and if we think deliberately, creatively, and strategically. This insight is a critically important life success lesson.

GETTING STARTED

It's now time to read the story. Depending on the reading level of your class, you may prefer to have students read the story aloud, or you may prefer to read the story to your students. Before beginning, take a look at the suggested questions that follow the story. You'll note that the instructional function of each question is indicated, and a general idea of the desired student response is provided. Be forewarned that you may not always get the desired response, and you may need to probe and guide children. This does not mean, however, that there is only one "right" answer. The objective is to train children to think analytically and to teach them how to solve the problems they're facing methodically and creatively. The process permits great instructional latitude. If the class discussion gets off to a rocky start, remind yourself that your students' critical and strategic thinking skills will improve incrementally. Be patient if children cannot immediately identify and comprehend the issues, perceive obvious links, and express their ideas. Analytical thinking is a skill, and as is the case when students are mastering any new skill, you must provide patient feedback, skilled guidance, repeated opportunities for practice, and affirmation for progress.

You many want to insert stopping points in the story so that you can ask questions that underscore the key points in the section just read. Gauge the situation. If your students seem anxious to react or comment or if their concentration begins to waver, stop and pose a thought-provoking question. Feel free to disregard any or all of the suggested questions at the end of the story and substitute your own. Go with the flow. If the discussion begins to lead in a productive direction that the suggested questions do not address, you may choose to follow that path.

Figure 1.2   Brainstorming Tree for Solving Problems (Sample)

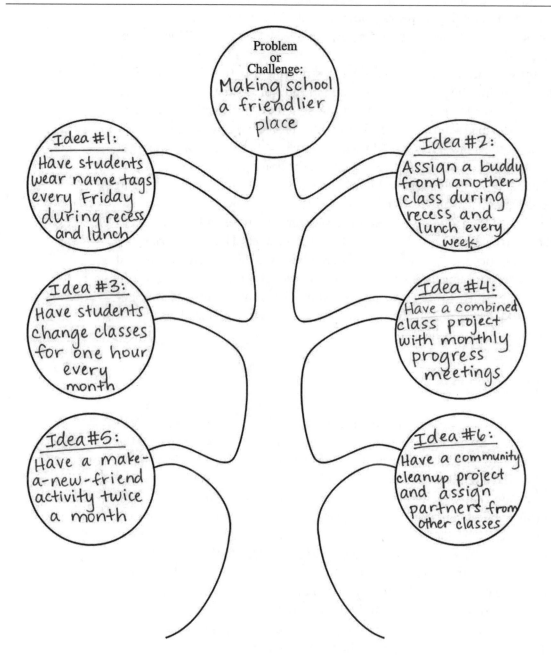

Have a community cleanup project and assign partners from other classes
Brainstormed Solution

For Students

The Child Who Doesn't Have Friends

THE STORY

1　It was just about time for recess, and the children were
2　very ready to go out to play. Tired from all the hard work
3　they had done, they were eager to have fun. As they waited
4　for the teacher's signal to line up, they could barely sit still.
5　"Please hurry up!" they thought as they sat impatiently at
6　their desks.

7　Finally, Ms. Bruxton told the students to line up at the
8　door. She put her finger to her lips. This was a signal they
9　knew very well. It meant no talking.

10　The children marched down the hall to the playground.
11　They knew that they weren't supposed to talk, but some
12　did anyway. When Ms. Bruxton heard them, she stopped
13　and turned around. She had a stern look on her face.
14　"Children, you know the rules," she said. "No talking in the
15　hall on the way to recess. Other children are still in class."
16　She again held her finger up to her lips. Everyone knew
17　that they had better be quiet.

18　When Ms. Bruxton opened the heavy door that led to
19　the playground, they all ran out.

20　Everyone except Justin was very excited. They were
21　free at last. They were all laughing and yelling and zoom-
22　ing everywhere. They knew that they had fifteen minutes
23　to play before they had to return to class.

24　Justin stood near the door and watched some boys
25　and girls run to get kickballs and basketballs. He saw

Ms. Bruxton reminding the children not to talk.

26 some children run to the swings, and others run to the
27 monkey bars. He watched as some played tag and hide-
28 and-seek and others played handball. He could see how
29 much fun they were having, hitting the big ball and bounc-
30 ing it against the wall.

31 Justin walked over to the fence. Everyone was playing
32 together in small groups, but no one asked him to join their
33 group. No one seemed to notice him as he wandered
34 around the playground. He felt sad and alone. It was as if
35 he weren't there. He thought about the word his father used
36 to describe the tiny insects they discovered under the tree
37 bark. His dad used the word *invisible.* He told Justin the
38 insects were so small that they almost couldn't be seen.
39 They were almost invisible. Justin felt like one of the tiny
40 insects under the tree bark. He felt invisible. It was as if no
41 one could see him, and no one knew that he was there.

42 Justin found a kickball and started bouncing it. Doing
43 something while the other children played together helped
44 him feel better. Bouncing the ball almost allowed him to
45 forget about being alone.

46 Justin finally got tired of bouncing the kickball. He fol-
47 lowed the fence as he walked around the edge of the play-
48 ground. None of the children paid any attention to him,
49 and no one talked to him. He was invisible.

Justin sitting alone while the other children play.

50 Ms. Bruxton came up to him and said, "Justin, why
51 don't you play with the other children?" Justin replied, "I
52 don't want to." He was lying. Ms. Bruxton looked sad. She
53 was about to say something when some boys started
54 chasing three girls. She turned and walked away to scold
55 them. Justin saw her shaking her finger at the boys.

56 After school, Justin went to the bus. He found an empty
57 seat at the back. He knew none of the children wanted
58 him to sit next to them. The other children were talking
59 together excitedly. Everyone was so glad that school was
60 over. They could go home and have milk and cookies and
61 then go out to play until they had to do their homework.

62 Justin knew that many of the children would get together
63 with friends who lived nearby. They would play at some-
64 one's house. He felt sad that his classmates never invited
65 him to their house to play.

66 Justin tried to figure out why he had no friends. He
67 couldn't come up with any reasons. Kids just didn't like him.

68 In the evening when Justin's family was sitting at the
69 dinner table, his mom or his dad would sometimes ask
70 him who his favorite friends were. Sometimes Justin
71 would tell them that he didn't have any friends. Sometimes
72 he would make up the names of pretend friends. When his

73 parents asked him why he didn't have any friends, Justin
74 would reply in a very low voice, "I don't know." He would
75 then stare at his plate. When his parents asked him more
76 questions, he would always respond, "I don't know."
77 Seeing that Justin didn't want to talk about not having
78 friends, they would change the subject.

79   Finally, after another lonely day in school, Justin
80 decided to talk with his dad when he came home from
81 work. "Nobody likes me. Nobody wants to be my friend,"
82 Justin blurted out with tears in his eyes. He started to cry.
83 His father put his arms around him. He sat down in the big
84 armchair in the living room and pulled Justin onto his lap.
85 He let Justin cry for a few minutes and just rubbed his
86 son's back. Mocha, Justin's black lab, came into the room
87 and lay down next to the armchair, resting her chin on the
88 floor between her paws. She seemed to sense that Justin
89 was upset, and she looked very sad.

90   "Justin, what do you like doing most of all?" his father
91 asked after Justin had stopped crying.

Justin telling his father his problem.

92 "I like looking for bugs. I like playing with my rock
93 collection. I like playing with Transformers. I like swinging
94 on the monkey bars," Justin replied.

95 "I have an idea," Justin's dad said. "I could to ask Ms.
96 Bruxton if she would be willing to make an announcement
97 to the class. I'll ask her to find out if there are any students
98 in the class who are interested in collecting bugs," Justin's
99 dad said. "She could ask the students who are interested
100 to come see her after class. She could help the kids start
101 a bug-collecting club. And you could join the club. Even if
102 there is only one other kid interested in collecting bugs,
103 you have enough for a club. You could go to the library
104 and find books on bugs. Maybe there's interesting stuff
105 you could look at on the Internet. You could have your club
106 meetings here or at someone else's house. What do think
107 of the idea?"

108 "I think it's good. But what happens if no one is
109 interested?'

110 "Let's see what happens. If no one is interested, you
111 might start a Transformer or a trading card club. Kids
112 could bring in their Transformers or cards to share with
113 each other. OK?"

114 "OK," Justin replied.

115 Justin wasn't sure the idea would work. He didn't think
116 that anyone would want to join the club if they knew he
117 would be in it. But his dad said, "All right, we'll give it a try.
118 I'll talk to Ms. Bruxton after school tomorrow."

ORAL QUESTIONS

Please note: As previously indicated, it's not necessary to pose all of the following questions for your students to derive full benefit from examining the story. Gear the examination process to the amount of time that you have available and to the maturity level, skill level, and focusing capacity of your class. Feel free to pick, choose, and substitute.

■ Why do you think that the other children might not want to play with Justin?

> **Function: *Developing analytical and critical thinking skills.***
>
> **Comments:** The types of responses you are looking for include:*
>
> - He doesn't seem interested in doing what other children enjoy doing.
> - He may not be good at the games they are playing.
> - He may be shy.
> - He may not know how to play the way other kids play.
> - He may not be fun to play with.
>
> *You don't need to elicit all of these reasons. Be prepared for off-target or illogical responses, which should be treated with sensitivity. As students participate in these class discussions, their reasoning and analytical thinking skills will improve. You want to create a safe context in which students feel that they can freely express their ideas and feelings.

■ What words would you use to describe Justin? Explain why you've chosen these words.

> **Function: *Developing observational skills, perceptiveness, and empathy.***
>
> **Comments:** The types of responses you are looking for include:
>
> - Shy
> - Timid
> - Lonely
> - Sad
> - Frightened
> - Different
> - Upset

■ Why do you think that Justin made up the story about his pretend friends?

Function: *Developing empathy.*

Comments: The types of responses you are looking for include:

- He didn't want his parents to know that he didn't have friends.
- He uses his pretend friends instead of real friends so that he doesn't feel lonely.
- His pretend friends will always accept him.
- His pretend friends will always be willing to play with him.

■ Do you have any ideas about how Justin might make friends?

Function: *Learning to brainstorm and problem solve. (It's recommended that you use the brainstorming tree [Figure 1.1] with students.)*

Comments: The types of responses you are looking for include:

- He could learn to play the games better.
- He could ask children to let him play with them.
- He could say hello to kids and be friendly.
- He could invite children to come to his house after school or over the weekend.
- He could choose a child he really wants to play with and ask if they could be friends.
- He could ask his dad to take him and another child to the movies or a baseball game.
- He could find someone who likes to do the same things he likes doing.

■ Why do you think Justin wants friends?

Function: *Enhancing analytical and critical thinking skills and empathy.*

Comments: The types of responses you are looking for include:

- It's fun to have friends and do things together.
- Playing isn't as much fun when you are alone.
- It's neat to be able to talk to friends about things.
- Friends make you feel liked and special.

■ Have you ever been lonely? If you have, describe when this happened and how you felt.

Function: *Enhancing analytical and critical thinking skills and empathy.*

Comments: The types of responses you are looking for include:

- When summer vacation started, I didn't see my friends as much and I felt sad and lonely.
- I went to camp and felt very homesick. I missed my mom and dad and my friends.
- My best friend went on vacation, and I missed her and felt very sad.
- My best friend moved to another state, and I had no one to play with.
- I broke my leg and had to stay home for two weeks. I felt very lonely.

■ Can you tell when another child is feeling sad? What might signal that the child is feeling sad?

Function: *Developing observational skills and enhancing sensitivity and empathy.*

Comments: The types of responses you are looking for include:

- An unhappy look on her face.
- Crying.
- Not wanting to play with other children.
- Not laughing at jokes.
- Not having friends.
- Looking lonely.

■ Do you have a friend who acts, looks, or dresses differently? If you do, describe your friend.

Function: *Developing heightened awareness and empathy.*

Comments: The types of responses you are looking for include:

- My friend is from India and is a Hindu. He goes to a temple instead of a church.
- My friend is from Thailand, and she has really pretty, special clothes that she wears on holidays.
- My friend uses an electric wheelchair. Sometimes she takes me for a ride.
- My friend is from Mexico, and his family eats very spicy food. It burns my tongue, but it tastes really good.

■ Why do you like this friend?

Function: *Developing analytical, evaluative, and expressive language skills.*

Comments: The types of responses you are looking for include:

- Her family acts differently from my family, and I learn new things when I am with her.
- I like to hear her talk in another language to her parents and brothers.
- When there are special Chinese holidays, my friend's family invites me to join them.
- My friend has a hearing problem, and she teaches me sign language.
- We play some fun games from my friend's country that kids don't play here.

■ What do you think of the idea that Justin's dad came up with to help his son make friends?

Function: *Developing analytical, evaluative, and critical thinking skills.*

Comments: The types of responses you are looking for include:

- I don't think it's a good idea because most kids don't like bugs.
- I think that there may be some kids who would join the club.
- I think starting a bug club could be fun.
- Starting a club could be neat, but I think they should choose a different type of club.

■ Is there anything besides helping Justin set up a bug club that the teacher might do to help Justin make friends?

Function: *Developing analytical, evaluative, strategic, critical thinking, and problem-solving skills.*

Comments: The types of responses you are looking for include:

- The teacher could talk to the class about being nice to kids who aren't invited to play.
- The teacher could punish children who are mean to other children.
- The teacher could team Justin with a buddy in class who likes the same things.
- The teacher could suggest kids who Justin's parents might call to set up playdates.

OPTIONAL ACTIVITY: CAREFUL
READING AND ANALYSIS OF THE STORY

(These exercises are designed for students who can read at the second-grade level and above.)

- Go back and look carefully at the story. Underline every sentence that describes how Justin felt as he wandered alone around the playground. (Hint: You can find the sentences in lines 31 to 41. You should be able to find two sentences.)
- Underline the sentence that describes how Justin felt when his classmates didn't invite him to their house to play. (Hint: There is one sentence, and you can find it in lines 62 to 65.)
- Underline every sentence in the story that describes what usually happens at the dinner table. (Hint: The sentences are in lines 68 to 78. See if you can find seven things that usually happen.)
- Justin told his dad how he felt. He said two things before he began to cry. Underline the two sentences in the story that describe how he felt. (Hint: You can find the sentences in lines 79 to 83.)
- Find and underline the sentences that describe the suggestions Justin's dad had for getting more information about bugs. (Hint: He had two suggestions, and you can find the sentences that contain these suggestions in lines 103 to 107.)
- Find and underline the sentences in the story that describe the other ideas Justin's dad had if no one in the class was interested in starting a bug club. (Hint: He had two other ideas, and you can find the sentences in lines 110 to 113.)
- Justin wasn't sure about whether the club idea would work. Find the sentence in the story that describes his concern and underline it. (Hint: You can find the sentence in lines 115 to 118.)

SUPPLEMENTAL REPRODUCIBLE EXERCISES

(These reinforcement exercises can be completed in class or assigned for homework.)

❑ **In the space below, write reasons a child might feel lonely.**

1. _____

2. _____

3. _____

4. _____

❑ **Rate the bug club idea that Justin's father suggested to help his son make friends.**

> **Learning to Use a Scale**
>
> Below you will find a *scale*. This scale is different from the one in your bathroom. It can be used to rate what you think about something. On this scale, **1 is poor, 5 is average, and 10 is excellent.** If you think an idea is *poor,* you would circle 1 or 2. If you think the idea is *below average,* you would circle 3 or 4. If you think the idea is *average or better than average,* you would circle 5, 6, or 7. If you think the idea is *good,* you would circle 8 or 9. If you think the idea is *great,* you would circle 10.

Choose the number that best describes how you rate the idea about starting a bug club.

1	2	3	4	5	6	7	8	9	10
Poor				Average					Excellent

❑ **Why did you choose the number you circled?**

_____

_____

_____

❑ **If you feel sad and lonely because you do not have friends, what could you do to fix the problem? Write your ideas in the space below.**

1. _____

2. _____

3. _____

4. _____

❑ **If you had a problem that was making you sad, would you be willing to talk to your parents or your teacher about it?   Yes   No**

❑ **Give the reasons why discussing problems with your parents or teacher could be helpful.**

1. _____

2. _____

3. _____

4. _____

❑ **Would you be willing to ask a child who you think feels lonely to play with you? Yes   No**

If you answered "yes," explain your reasons in the space below.

_____

_____

_____

If you answered "no," explain your reasons in the space below.

_____

_____

_____

FOLLOW-UP AND APPLICATION

Guiding children to expanded insight is a critically important step in teaching them how to fix problems and avoid crises. Making certain that they apply the insights and brainstormed ideas in the classroom and on the playground is an equally vital step.

Despite having examined in class the social issues raised in the story, you may not necessarily see immediate changes in your students' behavior. Habits can be difficult to break, and some youngsters may continue to be shunned by their classmates. For this reason, there must be follow-up. You'll want remind students of what they've learned about having friends, and you'll want to remind them to apply what they've learned when interacting with other children.

Socially alienated children should be identified and monitored. They should be tactfully alerted when they're acting inappropriately and diplomatically prompted to modify alienating behaviors. If they're hovering on the social periphery, you may need to gently prod them to participate in games of tag, handball, or dodgeball, and you may need to make certain that other children are treating them well.

At the same time, you must remind socially adjusted students about being kind, accepting, and sensitive to the feelings of children they invite to play with them. Remind them about how nice it would be if they would also choose to sit next to a lonely child on the school bus or to invite this child to their birthday party or to their home for a playdate. These reminders should be broached as suggestions. For reinforcement, you can refer to the class discussion and the brainstormed ideas that the class developed. This reinforcement is a critically important component in the cognitive behavioral modification model (see page xii). Changing entrenched negative behavior requires that children be provided with repeated opportunities to practice. The behavior altering process is akin to breaking in a new baseball glove. The glove needs to be oiled and repeatedly pounded until it fits well and becomes fully functional.

ADDITIONAL CONCRETE REINFORCEMENTS

As a class project, you might have children make posters that summarize what they've learned about making friends and about treating other children kindly. These posters will serve as tangible reminders. You can also point to the posters when you observe unacceptable behavior and, when appropriate, have children reread key points.

Another reinforcement would be to have students do skits that recap what they've discussed. In these skits, a popular student may play the role of a child who is rejected socially. Students would enact how they can be nice to other children who might be feeling rejected and lonely. For example, in the skit a group of children might pretend to be playing a game together. They see a child who is not participating in the game and who looks lonely, and they invite the child to join them. Students could create the dialogue for these skits.

Finally, you could design a special award that is given to the child who has shown kindness to another child during the past week. This award could be a small trophy that the rewarded child can keep on his or her desk for the entire week. The trophy could be passed on to another child the following week. You could select the child, or the class could nominate classmates by dropping names in a box and describing the nominees' acts of kindness. The selected child's name could also be added to a special poster.

Enhancing children's awareness, sensitivity, and empathy is unequivocally attainable. Improving children's manners and behavior is unequivocally doable. Strengthening children's problem-solving skills is unequivocally teachable. With effective instruction, guidance, and mentoring, achieving these objectives is virtually a "lock."

Unit 2

The Child Who Has Difficulty Learning

For Educators

*Examining the Emotional
Implications of Learning Problems*

Most students who struggle to learn are painfully aware of their academic deficiencies. When their learning deficits are extensive and cause them to stand out in the classroom, any belittling comments or derision from classmates are certain to have a devastating psychological impact. This disparagement cannot help but magnify the academically deficient student's embarrassment and feelings of inadequacy.

Despite the teacher's best efforts to discourage belittling reactions, an undercurrent of intolerance and insensitivity may persist. Children may laugh when the dyslexic student stumbles over words or repeatedly loses her place when reading aloud. They may groan when the ADHD child is inattentive, becomes confused, acts inappropriately, responds impulsively, or disrupts the class. They may snicker when the student with auditory processing deficits has difficulty understanding and following directions or when the inattentive child impulsively blurts out incorrect answers to questions.

Simply admonishing students who overtly or covertly demean their struggling classmates is not enough. The conduct simply cannot be tolerated, and the imposition of negative consequences for mean-spirited behavior is certainly appropriate. Far more can and should be done, however, to discourage the disparagement of academically challenged children. Students must be made aware of how they are treating their peers, and they must be sensitized to the profound impact that overt or covert ridicule can have on their classmates.

If left unchecked, unkindness and intolerance can become standard operating procedure for some children, and this conduct can spill over onto the playground and into the lunchroom. Even barely audible put-downs can be traumatic for struggling children and can further shred their already tenuous self-confidence. If the comments degenerate into malicious teasing and taunting, the psychological effects can be devastating. The emotionally vulnerable child who is on the receiving end of malevolent remarks such as, "You're really dumb!" is certain to cry inside. The child is also at risk for believing what she's told.

THE EFFECTS OF LEARNING DIFFERENCES

Students with significant learning problems are embroiled in a continual struggle to decode words accurately, comprehend content, retain information, follow written and verbal instructions, write legibly, express their thoughts on paper, master newly introduced skills, and keep up with their mainstream subjects. As these beleaguered students glance around the classroom and observe their classmates learning with seeming ease, they're apt to conclude that they're intrinsically and irreparably flawed.

For dyslexic students, the daily academic struggle involves trying to decipher words whose letters appear to have no connection to the way the words are pronounced. For children with poor hand-eye coordination and graphomotor deficits, forming legible and properly spaced letters that sit on the line represents monumental challenges. For those with visual and auditory discrimination and visual memory difficulties, spelling words accurately is a persistent nightmare. Being required to do math operations correctly, memorize number facts, edit and proofread written assignments, identify grammar and punctuation mistakes, write intelligible sentences, and pass tests is often an exhausting and overwhelming experience for the child who learns differently.

Accurately identifying students' learning deficits and providing effective specialized remedial assistance are clearly essential steps in getting the struggling child untracked, but despite the skillful intervention of dedicated and highly skilled school psychologists and resource specialists and the extra support from concerned classroom teachers, the academic deficiencies and challenges may persist. That frustrated and demoralized students often latch onto self-protecting and maladaptive attitudes and behaviors should come as no surprise.

CONDUCT COMMONLY ASSOCIATED WITH LEARNING PROBLEMS

The behaviors that academically deficient students typically use to insulate themselves from feeling inadequate include avoidance, helplessness, procrastination, blaming, resistance, or irresponsibility. Some children compensate for their learning difficulties by acting silly and immature, becoming aggressive, being disruptive, or assuming the role of class clown. Others escape into their daydreams and become withdrawn, passive, and unresponsive.

It would be misleading to imply that all children with learning differences develop maladaptive, ego-protecting behavior. Many academically deficient students are quite courageous and possess an indomitable spirit. These students continue to work conscientiously despite the formidable roadblocks they face in school. In most instances, their diligence and perseverance can be directly attributed to exceptional family support and exceptionally talented classroom teachers and resource specialists.

In the case of struggling students who do act in maladaptive ways, it's important to recognize that their counterproductive conduct is not causing their learning difficulties. Rather, this conduct is symptomatic of their learning difficulties, although it's certainly true that self-defeating behaviors and attitudes can amplify students' learning problems and pose monumental instructional challenges for the teacher. Patience and forbearance are vital, not only on the part of the teacher, but also, in many instances, on the part of the student's classmates, who may also be affected by the struggling student's conduct.

It's not uncommon for exasperated teachers who do not fully appreciate the implications of a learning dysfunction to conclude, "If only she would try harder and behave, she'd be able to do her work." On the surface, this conclusion may appear reasonable, but it's often based on a false premise, namely, that simply by trying harder the struggling child will be able to fulfill the requirements and keep up with the class. No one would dispute that effort and motivation are key factors in the academic achievement equation. A central question, however, must be addressed: Is the student doing poorly in school primarily because she's resistant and unmotivated, or is she doing poorly primarily because she's unable to do the assigned work and feels frustrated, discouraged, and incompetent? If the latter explanation is more accurate, then the need for effective remedial assistance, patience, tolerance, acknowledgment for effort, and affirmation for improvement is all the more vital during the transition from academic insufficiency to academic sufficiency. Should it become apparent that the learning assistance strategy is not working, the classroom teacher and the resource specialist must put their heads together to revise and reinvigorate the intervention plan.

Ideally, the remedial strategy should also include in-class activities specifically designed to help mainstreamed struggling students and their classmates recognize the emotional factors that may be driving any inappropriate conduct. Can children understand and relate to these underlying issues? The answer is unequivocally *yes!* All children have felt frustration, discouragement, resentment, anger, and envy from time to time and to varying degrees, and they've experienced firsthand the impact of these negative emotions.

That deportment problems can compound students' learning deficits and significantly complicate the challenges that classroom teachers face is beyond question. It's unrealistic, however, to expect academically demoralized youngsters to relinquish their ego-protecting armor until their learning difficulties are being addressed by an effective learning assistance strategy. Children who are frustrated, discouraged, and resistant must become convinced that they can actually win in school before they'll voluntarily relinquish their defensive attitudes and maladaptive behavior.

CLASSROOM SCRIPTS

Performance and behavioral scripts are usually quickly established in most classrooms. Students who excel academically are typically eager learners who delight in their academic successes. They master new skills with relative ease. They pay attention, follow directions, have a positive attitude, and take pride in their accomplishments. They submit neat, legible, and completed assignments.

They meet deadlines. They check over their work to eliminate careless mistakes. They are goal-driven and are highly responsive to recognition and affirmation for their successes. Their achievements generate pride in a job well done, and their accomplishments stimulate their motivation, effort, and diligence. Because these children feel confident and competent, they delight in reaching for the brass ring.

Struggling students are at the other end of the performance and attitude spectrum. They often have glaringly deficient skills. They typically learn passively, work inefficiently, and demonstrate marginal effort and motivation. Assignments are frequently incomplete and submitted late. Their work is also characteristically sloppy, illegible, and replete with errors. Many of these defeated learners appear content to coast through school in cerebral neutral and, unlike their achieving classmates, they often manifest little desire to reach for the brass ring. Instead, they grasp the vertical bar as the carousel turns, convinced that if they stretch too far, they'll fall off the horse.

Despite the best efforts of classroom teachers, resource specialists, and parents to provide remedial and emotional support, children who learn differently are clearly at risk for becoming psychologically bruised by negative school and playground experiences. It should not surprise us that struggling students frequently conclude that they're unintelligent, that school is "dumb," and that the skills and information being taught are useless.

Some students who are not achieving academically may be fortunate and possess other interests and talents. These youngsters may focus on these pursuits as an alternative to academic achievement. They may spend hours dribbling a basketball and shooting baskets, drawing pictures, skateboarding, playing video games, or jumping rope. They may decide that their ambition in life is to become a professional singer, athlete, musician, or actor, and they may convince themselves that they can do so without needing to know how to read, do math, or study productively. They may also conclude that to attain their goals, they don't have to graduate from high school. These illusions, of course, are destined to shatter. Children who fail to acquire functional academic skills are fated to experience painful reality checks down the road.

RESTRICTIVE ASSESSMENT CRITERIA

The traditional linking of performance and intelligence that students (and many teachers) use is beguilingly simple: Bright children do well in school and unintelligent children do poorly. This simplistic equation, however, fails to acknowledge a wide range of exceptional talents that may not necessarily manifest on the next spelling test or math quiz or even on the next IQ test.

The classic assessment paradigm—*superior ability = superior academic performance*—is lamentably flawed. In actuality, struggling students may be as bright or brighter than their academically achieving classmates, but because of their marginal scholastic performance, their actual capabilities may be overlooked or discounted.

One of the primary objectives of this unit is to help students who learn differently realize they are more capable than they may believe. This critically important insight can play a pivotal role in enhancing their self-confidence and self-esteem.

IDENTIFYING AND APPLYING MULTIPLE INTELLIGENCES

A Harvard professor named Howard Gardner has dramatically expanded the traditional paradigm for defining intelligence. He contends that there are many different types of intelligence that may be ignored by teachers in class and not assessed by traditional IQ tests. This expanded paradigm has particular relevance for students who learn differently because it can help struggling students and their teachers better appreciate capabilities that may currently be unacknowledged. The student who has difficulty reading may actually be brilliant in other areas that involve athletics, music, art, acting, or dance. The child may have exceptional reasoning or linguistic capabilities, or she may possess a natural ability to relate to others. Helping academically deficient students identify and capitalize on these potent but often unacknowledged manifestations of intelligence can provide an oasis in an otherwise barren and desolate scholastic desert. The discovery of heretofore unrecognized abilities can play a key role in stimulating children's thinking, helping them discover their interests, building their self-confidence, and encouraging them to develop talents that accentuate their strengths and not their weaknesses.

Coining the term *multiple intelligences,* Howard Gardner identified eight major areas of ability:

- **Verbal/Linguistic Intelligence:** Students possessing this type of intelligence have good auditory and verbal communication skills and use language to help them assimilate, comprehend, and retain information. They excel in class discussions, presentations, cooperative study groups, debates, and creative writing, and they enjoy telling stories and expressing their ideas. These students often gravitate to careers in law, writing, journalism, acting, teaching, or politics.
- **Visual/Spatial Intelligence:** Students possessing this type of intelligence have a talent for creating graphic images in their mind and on paper. Because they have a facility for visually conceptualizing and mentally imprinting what they see, these students prefer to assimilate and retain information by reading books and viewing charts, demonstrations, videos, maps, and movies. They tend to do well on tests that emphasize the recall of written information, and they often gravitate toward careers in areas such as engineering, mechanics, medicine, interior design, graphic arts, fine art, library research, or architecture.
- **Logical/Mathematical Intelligence:** Students possessing this type of intelligence feel comfortable and capable when using logic and reason. They tend to be more rational than emotional and have questioning minds. They like solving problems, doing puzzles, and figuring out "brain teasers." They are adept at using numbers and have a talent for linking pieces of information to form a whole. They enjoy classifying, categorizing, and doing calculations. Intrigued by the physical world, they enjoy experiments and demonstrations that help them understand what's

happening around them and the underlying factors causing these events. These students often gravitate toward careers in areas such as mathematics, engineering, geology, astronomy, theoretical science, applied and theoretical physical science, scientific research, teaching, medicine, computer hardware and software development, programming, or accountancy.

- **Interpersonal Intelligence:** Students possessing this type of intelligence are adept and comfortable in social situations. They're empathetic, try to see issues from another person's perspective, and are sensitive to what others think and feel. They find it easy to establish relationships, organize events, motivate people to work toward a common goal, resolve conflicts, build trust, maintain harmony, and encourage cooperation. These students often gravitate toward careers in areas such as sales, marketing, human resource development, management, advertising, psychology and counseling, or politics.

- **Intrapersonal Intelligence:** Students possessing this type of intelligence are likely to be introspective and aware of their feelings. Contemplative, interested in acquiring insights, and intent on understanding the dynamics of their relationships, these students often gravitate toward careers in areas such as clinical psychology, counseling, writing, religion, and teaching.

- **Bodily/Kinesthetic Intelligence:** Students possessing this type of intelligence are naturally coordinated and enjoy sports. They can control their movements (as in gymnastics, dancing, karate, ice skating, or basketball), have good gross-motor coordination and fine-motor dexterity, and excel in physical pursuits. They use movement to imprint information such as complex dance steps, a karate kick, or a gymnastic routine. These students capitalize on their natural bodily/kinesthetic intelligence and often gravitate toward careers in areas such as dance, athletics, acting, martial arts, sculpture, choreography, or coaching.

- **Musical/Rhythmic Intelligence:** Students possessing this type of intelligence have a natural talent for playing or composing music. They are highly responsive to rhythm, lyrics, melodies, and tonal patterns. They enjoy singing, playing musical instruments, performing on stage, marching in a band, and rehearsing. Adept at recalling melodies, the words to songs, and the notes in musical scores, they think in musical patterns and respond primarily to sounds. Students who capitalize on this type of natural intelligence often gravitate toward careers as singers, musicians, composers, conductors, disc jockeys, record producers, or music impresarios.

- **Naturalistic Intelligence:** Students possessing this type of intelligence enjoy interacting with animals, nature, and wildlife. They're interested in ecology, the environment, and the biological, chemical, and physical principles and phenomena that affect rain forests, oceans, jungles, seasonal cycles, animal reproduction, food chains, and species survival. Students who capitalize on this type of naturalistic intelligence often gravitate toward careers in botany, biology, oceanography, conservation, zoology, ecology, exploration, animal husbandry, veterinary medicine, zoo management, and forestry.

Students, of course, may possess more than one type of intelligence. For example, a child may have exceptional visual/spatial intelligence and may also be a talented natural athlete. In addition, she may possess superior logical/mathematical intelligence. In high school, she may excel in competitive volleyball and basketball, and in college, she may play varsity sports while majoring in biology. Upon completing college, she may decide to pursue a graduate degree in physiology while continuing to play team and individual sports whenever possible.

It may seem premature to encourage students in the primary grades to begin thinking about how their natural talents, aptitudes, and learning preferences might apply to specific vocations and careers. Certainly, the mastery of basic academic skills is still priority number one. At the same time, it's important to recognize that your students are beginning the process of figuring out who they are and what they do well. Of course, at this juncture, their conclusions are certainly not set in cement and may change. Nonetheless, helping students identify their intelligence type and encouraging them to deliberately avail themselves of their natural abilities could have a significant impact on their academic performance and be especially pivotal in the case of students who are struggling to learn.

Your goal is to help your students appreciate that people have different talents and learn in different ways. You also want to help your students realize that a certain academic subject may be easier for some students because they possess a particular type of intelligence, while other students may excel in different subjects because of their distinctive natural abilities. The key message you want to communicate is that one type of intelligence is not necessarily better than another type. Writing stories or understanding science may be easier for some, and drawing, doing math, or playing music may be easier for others. Helping students with learning differences understand this critically important concept can provide them with a vital psychological buffer against the tribulations that they encounter while struggling with the demands of the curriculum.

LEARNING PREFERENCES

In much the same way that students have preferences about colors, food, and clothing, so, too, are they likely to have conscious or unconscious learning preferences. Most successful students intuitively use their dominant and preferred learning modality or modalities when they learn. In contrast, struggling students typically fail to make the connection between academic success and the deliberate use of their learning preferences. These students don't realize that they can assimilate information and master skills most effectively when they deliberately utilize their learning strengths. They also don't realize that they can often use these natural capabilities to compensate for any deficiencies they may have. This is particularly relevant in the case of students with learning problems. Those who do not identify their learning preferences may continue to perform marginally despite any remedial assistance they receive.

You may be wondering whether young children can understand and relate to the concepts of learning preferences and multiple intelligences. Rest assured that they can, assuming the concepts are presented in age-appropriate language and sufficient concrete examples are presented.

Young children are aware that they're good athletes, good artists, or good singers. They may not be able to articulate their insights about their natural abilities, but on some level of consciousness, they realize that they prefer to listen to information rather than read about it or that they can better understand and remember information when it's communicated verbally. By identifying, acknowledging, and affirming your students' natural learning competencies, you are, in effect, saying to them, and especially to those who have learning problems, "Hey, you're OK! You have ability. Deliberately use your natural talents when you learn, and learning will be easier." Even young children can comprehend this logic.

Statements such as, "You do so well when you use your hands to do creative projects!" or "You have such wonderful natural ability in the area of music!" can go a long way toward improving the struggling student's feelings of adequacy. Such acknowledgment and affirmation also play an instrumental role in encouraging students to capitalize on their inherent talents.

Class discussions about how to identify and use natural learning strengths, preferences, and dominant learning style (i.e., auditory, visual, tactile, kinesthetic, experiential modalities, or a combination thereof) can play a key role in sustaining the effort and motivation of children who learn differently and in building their academic self-confidence and productive compensatory capabilities.

IDENTIFYING PREFERRED LEARNING MODALITIES

You can usually identify the preferred learning modality or modalities of your students by observing their modus operandi. Even children in first grade provide substantive clues about how they prefer to learn.

The following inventory is designed to help you uncover your students' learning preferences.

LEARNING MODALITY INVENTORY

	Yes	No	Not Sure
This student:			
1. Learns best by reading and seeing information.	____	____	____
2. Can understand and recall information best when seeing it in books or visually represented in diagrams, graphs, pictures, and charts.	____	____	____

3. Understands, learns, and retains information best by watching class presentations and demonstrations.   ____ ____ ____

4. Is more interested, motivated, and involved in learning when information is seen.   ____ ____ ____

5. Learns best by listening.   ____ ____ ____

6. Understands and remembers information best when it is verbally communicated.   ____ ____ ____

7. Enjoys participating in class discussions.   ____ ____ ____

8. Is more interested, motivated, and involved in learning when information is orally expressed.   ____ ____ ____

9. Learns best when activities are physical.   ____ ____ ____

10. Recalls and understands information best by manipulating models and tangible representations of data.   ____ ____ ____

11. Comprehends best when doing experiments, drawing pictures and diagrams, building models, and doing hands-on projects.   ____ ____ ____

12. Is more interested, motivated, and involved in learning when participating in physical activities such as dancing and sports.   ____ ____ ____

13. Learns best when using scissors and other tools.   ____ ____ ____

14. Can understand and recall how things work by touching and holding materials.   ____ ____ ____

15. Enjoys mechanical projects and can build, disassemble, and reassemble objects with little difficulty.   ____ ____ ____

16. Is more interested, motivated, and involved in learning when involved in hands-on projects.   ____ ____ ____

17. Likes to learn by figuring out how to do something independently.   ____ ____ ____

18. Enjoys learning through trial and error.   ____ ____ ____

19. Doesn't like to follow written or verbal instructions.   ____ ____ ____

20. Learns from mistakes and makes expedient adjustments to avoid repeating them.   ____ ____ ____

INTERPRETING THE SURVEY

Statements 1–4:   These statements relate to visual learning. If your responses to the statements in this area are primarily "yes," the student's learning preference is most likely visual.

Statements 5–8:   These statements relate to auditory learning. If your responses to the statements in this area are primarily "yes," the student's learning preference is most likely auditory.

Statements 9–12:   These statements relate to kinesthetic learning. If your responses to the questions in this area are primarily "yes," your student's learning preference is most likely kinesthetic.

Statements 13–16:   These statements relate to tactile learning. If your responses to the statements in this area are primarily "yes," your student's learning preference is most likely tactile. (Tactile and kinesthetic learning preferences often overlap.)

Statements 17–20:   These statements relate to experiential learning. If your responses to the statements in this area are primarily "yes," your student's learning preference is most likely experiential.

Because multiple intelligences and preferred learning modalities overlap, a student's dominant learning style is likely to correspond to his or her intelligence type. Students who possess superior verbal/linguistic intelligence should be encouraged to use the auditory modality when they learn, and those who possess superior visual/spatial intelligence should be encouraged to use the visual modality when they learn. Tactile and kinesthetic learners probably possess superior bodily/kinesthetic intelligence and whenever feasible they should be encouraged to capitalize on these capacities.

USING DOMINANT AND PREFERRED LEARNING MODALITIES

Auditory Learners assimilate information best by listening.

Characteristics: Auditory learners have a facility for comprehending and remembering verbal information. They enjoy class discussions and participating in study groups. They're able to remember the words to songs and the content of previous discussions, and they typically possess above-average verbal communication skills. They prefer to assimilate content by vocalizing or subvocalizing the information.

Tips for maximizing learning effectiveness: Auditory learners should be encouraged to recite information aloud until it's assimilated.

Visual Learners assimilate information best by seeing it.

Characteristics: Visual learners have an advantage when learning and recalling facts and data written in books. They can typically "see" the correct spelling of words in their mind, and because of this capability, visual learners are usually good spellers. When they proofread, they can catch many of their own misspellings because "the word just doesn't *look* right." They are adept at recalling written telephone numbers, math facts, people's faces, written directions, data in diagrams and graphs, and information in newspaper and TV ads.

Tips for maximizing learning effectiveness: Visual learners should be encouraged to read content multiple times until they assimilate it. They should be urged to associate learning with using a camera to take a picture. Their eyes are the camera lens, and their brain is the film or digital chip on which they imprint information. Whenever feasible, visual learners should be encouraged to use diagrams, illustrations, graphs, charts, and flash cards as study tools.

Kinesthetic Learners assimilate information best by linking the data with movement.

Characteristics: Kinesthetic learners excel when activities involve physical movement. They can recall and understand information better when they involve their body and movement in the learning process. They learn best by creating projects and using tools. They delight in mastering skills through practice and repetition. The skills then become automatic and visceral and appear to bypass conscious thought.

Tips for maximizing learning effectiveness: Kinesthetic learners should be encouraged to assimilate information through movement, and, whenever possible, they should incorporate physical activity when they assimilate academic content. For example, they might tap out the beat of poem that they are memorizing or create a physical pattern or rhythm for learning math facts.

Tactile Learners assimilate information best by touching and manipulating materials.

Characteristics: Tactile learners learn best when they are able to take part in hands-on learning. For example, they might use or build a model of what they are required to learn. They also enjoy doing experiments and classification activities and excel when designing and constructing three-dimensional projects. Because making information tangible may not always be feasible or sufficient, tactile learners must also learn to use other learning modalities if they are to be successful in most upper-level academic subjects.

Tips for maximizing studying and learning effectiveness: Tactile learners should be encouraged to assimilate information through hands-on manipulation of tangible materials and should translate data into concrete representations.

Experiential Learners assimilate information best by applying and doing.

Characteristics: Experiential learners excel when they are involved in hands-on learning and share key characteristics with tactile learners and kinesthetic learners. They enjoy physical science, experimentation, and technology. Learning as they go, they derive insight from both their positive and negative experiences. Hands-on experiences help them understand, link, and recall data and concepts. Whenever feasible, these students should be urged to make information concrete. Despite their preference for dealing with the tangible, experiential learners must also be able to use other learning modalities to understand and recall textbook content.

Tips for maximizing learning effectiveness: Experiential learners should be encouraged to assimilate information through experimentation and trial and error. Combining experiential learning with tactile and kinesthetic learning (e.g., taking something apart to figure out how the pieces fit together) can enhance academic content assimilation and mastery.

EXAMINING THE STORY

The description of the distress that Ashley, the student highlighted in the following anecdote, experiences is all but certain to resonate in children who identify with her plight. The story is intended to help struggling students acquire greater insight about their problems and the feelings that are associated with these feelings. The story is also designed to help other students in the class acquire more compassion for the challenges that students with learning differences face every day.

The anecdote describes the day-in and day-out anxiety, frustration, and demoralization that are often standard fare for children with learning problems. Ashley's experiences are likely to be shared to varying degrees by virtually all academically deficient students, and these children are likely to relate immediately to her frustration, sadness, and self-consciousness.

The story examines core issues associated with learning differences. It also delivers a positive message, namely, that with appropriate help and effort, students can handle their learning problems and, in many cases, prevail over them. This realization can be a major morale booster for the demoralized child.

The story and the questions that follow it are not exclusively directed at academically deficient students. The content also targets successful students who are unaware of the pain that unkindness and insensitivity can trigger in children who are battling to learn. The goal is to make your students more cognizant, considerate, and empathetic to the tribulations some of their classmates may be experiencing. The operating premise is that with guidance and opportunities for practice, feedback, and encouragement, young children can be taught to be kinder and more compassionate.

Because you may not necessarily choose to present the units in the order in which they are presented, you may find it beneficial to refer to the general instructional suggestions described on pages 10 through 13 in Unit 1. These recommendations are relevant to all of the units in the program.

THE QUESTIONS THAT FOLLOW THE STORY

As noted in Unit 1, it isn't necessary to ask all of the questions that are posed in the section that directly follows the story. You want to avoid giving your students the impression that they're being interrogated. The questions are designed to be a catalyst for discussion and interaction. Time considerations may necessitate your limiting the number of issues that are examined in class, so feel free to pick and choose. Your goal is to expand your students' awareness and insight by encouraging the development of analytical thinking, strategic thinking, critical thinking, and problem-solving skills.

Be prepared to acknowledge and affirm your students' feelings and ideas even if they are off target. If you conclude that students are not "getting it," you might redirect their thinking by suggesting another way of looking at an issue. For example, you might say, "What do you think about this idea?" As suggested in Unit 1, you may want to have students use the brainstorming tree to summarize the problem-solving process (see discussion and diagrams on pages 11–14). You may also find it useful to review the suggestions on pages 10 through 11 about communicating to your students that you're genuinely interested in what they're saying and that you appreciate their willingness to share their ideas and feelings.

It's time to examine the story and to do the exercises and activities with your class. You may decide to read the story aloud to your class, or you may want your students to read the story aloud.

For Students

The Child Who Has Difficulty Learning

THE STORY

1   Ashley was so nervous that she could barely sit still.
2 Her mouth felt as if it were stuffed with cotton balls. As she
3 waited for her turn to read, her heart was beating, and her
4 body was trembling. There were only two more children
5 ahead of her, and then it would be her turn to read.

6   Ashley knew what would happen next. She would
7 make a mistake, and some kids would begin to giggle.
8 They wouldn't actually laugh loud enough for Ms.
9 Goldman to hear because they knew that she would get
10 mad. The giggling, however, would be just loud enough for
11 Ashley to hear. It would cause her to become so nervous
12 that she would make even more reading mistakes.

13   When Ashley tried to sound out the words, they often
14 didn't make any sense. As she became more and more
15 frustrated and upset, she would start to have trouble read-
16 ing even the easy words. Although Ms. Goldman would
17 help her, Ashley could still hear some children groaning
18 each time she made a mistake. If Ms. Goldman heard
19 children make fun of her, she would tell them to stop, but
20 by then it would be too late. By this point Ashley would
21 usually be so confused that she would lose her place and
22 begin reading the same words over again. She would
23 leave out words and skip lines. She would read the word
24 "pat" as "tap" or the word "saw" as "was." She would con-
25 fuse "bad" and "dad." Then her brain would stop working,
26 and Ms. Goldman would have to help her with almost
27 every word.

28   By the middle of first grade, Ashley hated reading. She
29 especially disliked reading aloud. She felt it was so unfair
30 that she had so much difficulty sounding out words and
31 the other kids didn't. Ashley was convinced that she
32 couldn't read well because she was "dumb." That's what
33 some children would call her on the playground. They
34 would say, "You're so dumb, you can't even read!" When
35 they said this, Ashley's cheeks would start burning, and
36 she would want to run away and hide. But there was
37 nowhere to really hide on the playground, and Ashley
38 would just walk away from the children who were making
39 fun of her. She would feel very sad, and tears would well
40 up in her eyes.

41   As the student sitting in front of her began to read
42 aloud, Ashley felt her heart pounding like a drum. She was
43 next! Ashley had allowed her mind to wander while
44 Jessica was reading, and she hadn't followed along. She
45 desperately tried to find her place in the book, and she
46 was certain everyone was staring at her. "Which sentence
47 is Jessica reading?" a voice screamed inside her head.

48   When it was finally her turn to read, Ms. Goldman had
49 to help her find where to start. Ashley could hear the child

Ashley waiting for her turn to read.

50 next to her laugh. This made her so upset that she could
51 barely make out the words on she page.

52   Ashley was getting help from the resource specialist,
53 but it didn't seem to make any difference. She still made
54 mistakes when she read. She still had difficulty doing
55 math problems. She still had difficulty getting her words to
56 sit on the line when she wrote. Her spelling tests and
57 homework assignments still had red marks all over them.
58 Everything seemed hopeless, and Ashley was convinced
59 that she wasn't making any progress. She was just too
60 dumb. She hated school!

61   "Why go to school at all?" Ashley often asked herself.
62 She had decided that she wanted to become a famous
63 actress, and she was certain she didn't need to know how
64 to read or do math to act in movies or on TV. She didn't need
65 to know about stupid science or history. So what if kids
66 laughed at her? She'd show them. One day her classmates
67 would see her in a movie. She would be famous, and they
68 would feel bad because they made fun of her in school.

69   As usual, it took forever for school to end. Finally, the
70 bell rang, and Ashley was free. She had somehow made
71 it through another awful day.

72   Ashley ran to the bus and was the first one in line. She
73 climbed up the steps and chose a seat by the window.
74 She then waited impatiently for the bus to leave. She
75 wanted to get home so she could watch her favorite car-
76 toons. If the bus left on time, she would be home by 3:30.
77 That would give her an hour and a half of TV before the
78 adult programs started.

79   Ashley had made a deal with her mother. She could
80 watch TV after school until 5:00, or she could play. Then
81 she would have to do her homework until dinnertime at
82 6:00. Any homework that was left over had to be finished
83 immediately after dinner.

84   At 5:00 every afternoon, Ashley and her mom would
85 usually have an argument. Ashley hated homework, and
86 there was always something she would rather do instead.
87 She'd begin playing with Murphy, her dog, or she'd turn

Ashley playing with her dog instead of studying.

88 the TV back on, even though she knew she wasn't sup-
89 posed to. Then her mother would tell her that she needed
90 to get down to work. Usually, Ashley would continue to fool
91 around. Her mom would accuse her of procrastinating and
92 threaten not to let her watch any TV that evening. It was
93 so unfair!

94 After putting off her work for as long as she could,
95 Ashley finally opened her math book and took out a piece
96 of paper from her binder. She stared at the page of addi-
97 tion problems for a few minutes, but her mind was a mil-
98 lion miles away. Then she began to doodle on her paper.
99 She drew arrows and five-pointed stars, and then she
100 drew squiggly lines connecting the arrows and stars. All of
101 a sudden, she heard her mother's voice coming from the
102 kitchen.

103 "Are you getting your work done, Ashley?" she asked.

104 "Yes," Ashley replied in an irritated tone of voice. Of
105 course, this wasn't really the truth.

106 Ashley's mother came to the door of her room a few
107 moments later. She was holding a big spoon in her hand.

108 "Dinner will be ready in thirty minutes. I expect you to
109 have your math problems done before we sit down. And I
110 want you to begin studying your spelling words for the test
111 on Friday," she said with a firm voice. "I'll quiz you on them
112 after dinner."

113 "I'll start studying the spelling words tomorrow. The test
114 isn't for three days," Ashley replied with frustration.

115 "You need to start studying your spelling words now.
116 You know that it takes you extra time to learn them."

117 Ashley sighed. Her mother was always bugging her
118 about studying. After dinner her mom would sit with her at
119 the kitchen table and help her with her reading assign-
120 ment. Then she would test her on her spelling words. It
121 was so boring. None of the words would sit still on the
122 page when she tried to read. They danced around and
123 gave her a headache. The p's, g's, q's, d's, and b's all
124 looked alike to her. The same thing also happened when
125 she was doing math. 9's looked like 6's. And she would
126 often write her 2's, 4's, 5's, and 7's backward. Because
127 she had difficulty lining up the number columns when she
128 added and subtracted, she often got the wrong answer.
129 Her teacher would put lots of red marks on her papers,
130 which the other kids could see when her work was
131 handed back to her. This made her feel so embarrassed,
132 she wanted to run out of the classroom. Ashley always did
133 terribly on spelling tests. No matter how hard she studied,
134 she would misspell most of the words. She would even
135 misspell the words that she got right on the practice tests
136 her mother gave her at home.

137 "I'm going to fail the test anyway, so why study the
138 spelling words?" Ashley thought angrily. "And why should
139 I do the math problems if my answers are always wrong?"

140 To make matters worse, when Ashley was out of the
141 classroom working with the resource specialist, she would
142 miss the work being done in her regular class. This would
143 cause her to fall even farther behind. Everything seemed
144 hopeless.

145   "Dinner's ready!" Ashley's mother finally called.

146   "I'm coming," Ashley yelled as she got up from her desk.

147   Ashley hadn't finished her math problems and hadn't
148   started studying her spelling words. She knew that her
149   mother would ask about how much work she had done. If
150   she didn't tell the truth, her mom would be mad. If she did
151   tell the truth about how little work she had completed, her
152   mom would be mad, too. Ashley felt like she couldn't win
153   no matter what she did.

154   When Ashley's mom asked about her homework,
155   Ashley just looked at her plate and said nothing. She could
156   tell from the expression on her mother's face that she
157   was upset with her. Ashley then listened silently as her
158   older sister, Caitlin, bragged about the A's she had gotten
159   on her science test and her book report. The bragging
160   made Ashley very mad, but she didn't say anything.

Caitlin's report card.

161   After the girls had cleared the table and loaded the
162   dishwasher, Caitlin went to her room to finish her home-
163   work. Ashley's mother pointed to a chair at the kitchen
164   table and asked Ashley to sit down.

165 "I know that I get upset with you when you don't do
166 your work," Ashley's mom said. "It bothers me when you
167 don't try hard, but I also understand that the work is very
168 difficult for you."

169 "I hate school!" Ashley blurted out. "The kids laugh at
170 me when I read aloud and make mistakes. And when I go
171 to the chalkboard to do a math problem, they think I'm
172 dumb because I never get the answer right." Tears were
173 rolling down her cheeks.

174 "Does your teacher let the children laugh at you?"
175 Ashley's mother asked gently.

176 "She gets mad at them, but they laugh anyway," Ashley
177 replied bitterly.

178 "Do you see any way to deal with the problem?" her
179 mom asked in a gentle voice.

180 "No," Ashley sobbed.

181 "Well, honey, let's see if we can come up with some
182 solutions to the problem. I know that you believe you
183 aren't making any progress. I think that you are showing
184 improvement. We just need to speed up the progress so
185 that you don't feel so discouraged. I had a meeting at
186 school this afternoon with your resource specialist, and
187 she's agreed to spend more time with you. She's also
188 going to use a special new program to help you with your
189 reading, and she is going to help you figure out how you
190 learn best. Then you'll be able to use your learning
191 strengths to help you keep up in class. I've also decided
192 to hire a tutor to help you with your reading, math, and
193 homework. During the summer, you'll continue to work
194 with the tutor several hours a week so that you can catch
195 up. With the extra help, I'm certain that school will become
196 easier for you. It won't happen overnight, but it will hap-
197 pen. What do you think of the plan?"

198 "I don't know," Ashley replied in a low voice.

199   "You're going to get this problem solved. Be patient,
200 honey. You're going to win this battle. I'm also going to
201 speak to Ms. Goldman about the children who are laugh-
202 ing at you in class and making fun of you on the play-
203 ground. I'm sure that she'll deal with this."

204   "OK," Ashley said, again in a low voice. She wanted to
205 believe her mother, but she wasn't sure the plan would
206 work. Still, just knowing that there was a new plan that
207 could work made her feel better. She'd just have to wait
208 and see.

ORAL QUESTIONS

■ Why do you think that other children make fun of Ashley?

> **Function: *Developing analytical and critical thinking skills.***
>
> **Comments:** The types of responses you're looking for include:*
>
> - She makes lots of mistakes in class.
> - She has trouble reading words that are really easy.
> - She loses her place when she reads.
> - She doesn't seem to be trying very hard.
>
> *You don't need to elicit all of these reasons. Be prepared for off-target or illogical responses, which should obviously be treated with sensitivity. As students participate in these class discussions, their reasoning and analytical thinking skills will improve. You want to create a safe context in which students feel that they can freely express their ideas and feelings.

■ What words would you use to describe Ashley? Explain why you've chosen these words.

> **Function: *Developing observational skills, perceptiveness, and empathy.***
>
> **Comments:** The types of responses you're looking for include:
>
> - Upset
> - Unsure of herself
> - Sad
> - Discouraged
> - Frustrated
> - Angry

■ Why do you think Ashley hates school?

> **Function: *Developing analytical thinking skills and empathy.***
>
> **Comments:** The types of responses you're looking for include:
>
> - The work is very difficult for her.
> - She can't read the words.
> - She feels frustrated
> - It doesn't seem to make any difference whether or not she tries hard.
> - Children laugh at her when she makes mistakes in class.
> - Children tease her on the playground and tell her she's dumb.
> - Her mom always keeps after her to do her homework.

■ Do you have any ideas about how Ashley might handle her classmates' giggling, laughing, and teasing?

Function: *Learning to brainstorm and problem solve (see Figure 1.1., the brainstorming tree, page 12).*

Comments: The types of responses you're looking for include:

- She could tell the teacher that the giggling, laughing, and teasing are bothering her.
- She could ask the teacher to tell her the day before what paragraph she would have to read in class, and she could practice reading it with the teacher or her mom.
- She could discuss the problem with her special reading teacher.
- She could concentrate more so that she doesn't lose her place.

■ What might cause Ashley to feel unintelligent?

Function: *Enhancing analytical and critical thinking skills and empathy.*

Comments: The types of responses you're looking for include:

- She has difficulty learning new information.
- She makes mistakes when she's reading aloud or doing math problems at the chalkboard.
- She has difficulty reading even easy words.
- Kids laugh at her in class when she reads aloud.
- Kids tease her on the playground.
- Her sister is a good student.
- She doesn't think she's making any improvement.

■ Why do you think Ashley puts off doing her homework?

Function: *Enhancing analytical and critical thinking skills and empathy.*

Comments: The types of responses you're looking for include:

- She finds the homework very difficult.
- She's frustrated.
- She's angry about having to do her homework.
- Doing homework makes her feel dumb.
- Even if she studies her spelling words, she gets them wrong on the quiz.
- Even if she does her homework, she knows she'll make lots of mistakes.

■ How would you feel if children laugh at you while you're reading in class?

Function: *Developing analytical thinking skills and enhancing sensitivity, empathy, and compassion.*

Comments: The types of responses you're looking for include:

- I would feel angry.
- I would feel that I'm not smart.
- I would feel embarrassed.
- I would feel upset.
- I would feel that the other children didn't like me.
- I would think that my reading problems couldn't be fixed.

■ How could Ashley show that she's intelligent even though she has a learning problem? Can you think of ways that don't involve reading, math, or spelling?

Function: *Developing analytical thinking skills and heightened awareness and insight.*

Comments: The types of responses you're looking for include:

- She could be good artist.
- She could be a good dancer.
- She could be a good athlete.
- She could be a good actor.
- She could be a good singer.
- She could be a good musician.*

* Please refer to discussion of multiple intelligences on pages 35–37.

■ Why do you think Ashley's mother pesters her about her homework?

Function: *Developing analytical, evaluative, and expressive language skills.*

Comments: The types of responses you're looking for include:

- She feels that Ashley is wasting time.
- She feels Ashley is not working hard.
- She's concerned that Ashley won't complete her homework.
- She wants Ashley to try harder.
- She wants Ashley to do better in school.

■ What do you think of the ideas that Ashley's mom has for helping her daughter do better in school?

Function: *Developing analytical, evaluative, and critical thinking skills.*

Comments: The types of responses you're looking for include:

- I think they're good ideas because if she gets more help, she'll do better in school.
- The special program could help her make more progress.
- Getting help during the summer will help her catch up and do better next year.
- Talking to the teacher and asking her to make sure the kids don't laugh at Ashley is a good idea because then Ashley won't feel embarrassed and sad.

■ Are there any other ideas that could help Ashley improve her schoolwork and feel better about herself?

Function: *Developing analytical, evaluative, strategic, critical thinking and problem-solving skills.*

Comments: The types of responses you're looking for include:

- The teacher could ask children in the class to help Ashley with her work in class.
- The teacher could punish children who make fun or laugh at Ashley.
- The teacher could team Ashley with a buddy who could help her.
- The teacher could give Ashley easier assignments until she catches up.
- The teacher could ask Ashley questions in class that she can answer.
- The teacher could have Ashley do projects that she can complete and then let her show off her work to the other kids.

■ If Ashley was in your class, what could you do to help her feel better about herself?

Function: *Developing analytical, evaluative, and critical thinking skills and empathy.*

Comments: The types of responses you're looking for include:

- I could offer to help her if she was having difficulty with her homework.
- I could let her know that I like her.
- I could decide never to giggle or laugh if she makes a mistake in class.
- I could invite her to play with me during recess.
- I could have playdates with her after school and during the weekends.
- I could invite her to my birthday party.

OPTIONAL ACTIVITY: CAREFUL READING AND ANALYSIS OF THE STORY

(These exercises are designed for students who can read at the second-grade level and above.)

- Go back and look carefully at the story. Underline every sentence that describes how Ashley felt as she was waiting to read aloud in class. (Hint: You can find the sentences in lines 1 to 4. You should be able to find two sentences.)
- Underline the sentence that describes how Ashley felt when children giggled or laughed after she made mistakes while reading. (Hint: You can find the sentence in lines 9 to 12.)
- Underline every sentence in the story that describes the types of mistakes that Ashley made when she was reading. (Hint: There are lots of sentences that describe Ashley's reading problems. See if you can find at least eight sentences in lines 11 to 27.)
- Underline the sentence that describes what the children called Ashley on the playground. (Hint: You can find the sentence in lines 31 to 36.)
- Find and underline the sentences that describe what Ashley did when the children made fun of her on the playground and how she felt. (Hint: You can find the three sentences in lines 36 to 40.)
- Find and underline the sentences in the story that describe the other areas in which Ashley was having difficulty in school. (Hint: There are three sentences that describe the problem areas, and you can find these sentences in lines 53 to 57.)
- Find and underline the two sentences that describe what happened when Ashley sat down to do her math homework. (Hint: You can find the sentences in lines 96 to 102.)
- Ashley wasn't sure about whether her mom's plan to help her make more progress in school would work. Find the sentence in the story that describes her feelings about the plan, and underline it. (Hint: You can find the sentence in lines 204 to 206.)

SUPPLEMENTAL REPRODUCIBLE EXERCISES

(These reinforcement exercises can be completed in class or assigned for homework.)

❏ **In the space below, write reasons a child might feel sad if she is struggling in school.**

1. _____

2. _____

3. _____

4. _____

❏ **Choose the number that best describes how you rate the plan that Ashley's mother came up with to help Ashley improve her schoolwork.**

1	2	3	4	5	6	7	8	9	10
Poor				**Average**					**Excellent**

Using a Scale

If you've forgotten how to rate something using a scale, look back on page 25.

❏ **Choose the number that best describes how you rate the idea of Ashley spending more time with the resource specialist.**

1	2	3	4	5	6	7	8	9	10
Poor				**Average**					**Excellent**

❏ **Why did you choose the number you circled?**

_____

_____

_____

❏ **Choose the number that best describes how you rate the idea of hiring a tutor to help Ashley with her reading, math, and homework.**

1	2	3	4	5	6	7	8	9	10
Poor				**Average**					**Excellent**

❏ **Why did you choose the number that you circled?**

_____

_____

_____

❏ **Choose the number that best describes how you rate the idea of Ashley spending a few hours each week during the summer working with a tutor to catch up with the class.**

1	2	3	4	5	6	7	8	9	10
Poor				**Average**					**Excellent**

❑ **Why did you choose the number you circled?**

_____

_____

_____

❑ **If you feel sad because you are having difficulty with something in school, what could you do to fix the problem? Write your ideas in the space below.**

1. _____

2. _____

3. _____

4. _____

❑ **If you feel sad because children are teasing you or making fun of you, would you be willing to talk to your parents or your teacher about it?   Yes   No**

❑ **Give the reasons why discussing the problem with your parents or teacher could be helpful.**

1. _____

2. _____

3. _____

4. _____

❑ **Would you be willing to ask a child who is being made fun of in school because of learning problems to play with you during recess or after school?   Yes   No**

If you answered "yes," explain your reasons in the space below.

_____

_____

_____

If you answered "no," explain your reasons in the space below.

_____

_____

_____

FOLLOW-UP AND APPLICATION

Guiding students to greater insight is a critically important step in the process of teaching them how to fix problems and avoid crises. Making certain that they apply the insights and brainstormed ideas that they acquired from examining the anecdote and participating in the class discussion both in the classroom and on the playground is equally important.

Despite having examined in class the issues related to classmates who may have learning differences (or other types of differences), you may not necessarily see immediate and dramatic changes in some students' behavior vis-à-vis the struggling children in class. Some students may continue to be insensitive and disparaging to classmates who are having academic difficulties.

Behavior patterns can be difficult to break, and for this reason, there should be follow-up and reinforcement. You'll want to remind students about what it means to be compassionate. You'll want to remind your students about the importance of being kind and supportive of other children with learning differences. Students should be alerted when you see or hear them hurting another child's feelings, and they should be unequivocally discouraged from resorting to disparaging behavior. They must be repeatedly prompted to treat their classmates with kindness until this critically important message is assimilated.

You want your students to realize how nice it would be if they were to choose to sit next to a child on the school bus who is struggling in class or to invite this child to their birthday party or to their home for a playdate. These prompts should be broached as suggestions. To make your point, you can refer to the class discussion and the brainstormed ideas that the class developed. This reinforcement is a key component in the cognitive behavioral change model that is used throughout this program (see page xii). Changing negative behaviors requires that students be guided, mentored, and monitored.

Students must be reminded of the impact of their conduct on their classmates, and they must be furnished with opportunities to practice positive behaviors. Providing effusive acknowledgment and praise for behavioral changes is a critical component in the cognitive behavioral change process. Although it may not always seem so on trying days, the vast majority of your students actually do want to please you, and they crave your affirmation. You cannot assume that they necessarily know how to earn this approval, however obvious the cause-and-effect equation may seem. You must tell them what you value!

CONCRETE REINFORCEMENTS

As a class project, you might have students create posters that summarize what they've learned about being kind to children who have learning differences. These posters would serve as tangible reminders of the issues that they've examined in class. You can also point to the posters when you observe students' unacceptable responses to the tribulations of struggling classmates. When appropriate, you may have children reread the key points aloud.

Another reinforcement could involve having students do skits that recap what they've discussed. In these skits, students could enact how they can help and be nice to children who are struggling in school. For example, in the skit a group of children might pretend to be reading, and one child may be struggling when it's her turn to read. (Select a child to play this part who doesn't actually have a reading problem.) Children might suggest ways in which they could assist and support the struggling child.

Enhancing your student's empathy for classmates who learn differently and altering their manners, behavior, and attitudes are unequivocally attainable objectives. Strengthening their analytical and strategic thinking and problem-solving skills and helping them become more aware and empathetic are also unequivocally attainable objectives. With effective instruction, guidance, mentoring, acknowledgment, and affirmation for progress, your students can become more aware and compassionate. These youngsters will evolve into better and more sensate human beings. It's guaranteed.

Unit 3

The Child
Who Steals

For Educators

*Examining the Dynamics
and Implications of Stealing*

Children's behavior provides a portal into the underlying feelings and thoughts that impel their actions. When children steal and the conduct is chronic, something is amiss. Red flags are flapping, and these warning signals must be heeded and addressed.

The traditional explanation for stealing is that core values and rules about honesty either haven't been adequately taught at home or haven't been assimilated. These explanations may be accurate, but they may also be overly simplistic.

Young children are programmed by nature to be both inquisitive and acquisitive. Their natural curiosity and desire to possess objects that attract their attention can be compelling, especially at the toddler and preschool stages of development. Because the capacity to self-regulate is not yet developed, young children may brazenly pick up and walk off with items that pique their interest irrespective of who owns these items. While playing in a sandbox, a three-year-old may brashly appropriate another child's toy truck. He may impulsively reach for a candy bar at the supermarket checkout counter simply because he wants it. When instructed to return the purloined object, the child may become indignant and resistant. From the child's narcissistic perspective, the object belongs to him simply because he desires it and feels entitled to it. For the same reason, a four-year-old may take a shiny tool from his father's workbench or a gleaming piece of jewelry from his mother's jewelry box, and a five-year-old may abscond with a doll that belongs to her older sister. At this early stage of development, egocentricity is a dominant force. The boundaries that delineate acceptable from unacceptable behavior are not yet fully established, and an appreciation for the social conventions regarding ownership are not yet fully understood or internalized.

Most parents handle their child's unacceptable acquisitive behavior with firm and consistent reminders about the rules and with appropriate rebukes for transgressions. "You may not take something that that doesn't belong to you without permission" is one of the common parental litanies during the formative years.

Wise parents realize they must repeatedly define and clarify the limits of socially acceptable behavior, and they must continually exhort their child to abide by these restrictions. This process of deliberately and methodically setting limits is one of parents' most compelling responsibilities. The challenges that parents face when establishing these boundaries vary from child to child. Some children internalize the restrictions effortlessly. Others require a more intensive process of defining, clarifying, reminding, and enforcing the regulations. The goal of this methodical values training is to help children integrate the basic principles of honesty and accountability and to help them develop inhibition, a fundamental requisite to effective societal functioning.

Children must be conditioned to control their impulses, resist detrimental temptations, use good judgment, and obey the rules. If they fail to assimilate the core do's and don'ts, they're likely to experience painful collisions and reality checks down the road. The sooner children acquire context- and age-appropriate self-control, the easier their lives will be.

By the age of six, most children have ideally learned that taking other people's possessions won't be tolerated at home, in the classroom, and on the playground. Occasional lapses may still occur, but by this stage youngsters should have assimilated the requisite impulse control for successful accommodation to in-school and out-of-school conventions about stealing. They should also be aware of basic cause-and-effect principles and should realize that there will be unpleasant consequences if they take other people's possessions without permission. Their parents and teachers are certain to become upset and mete out punishments for the transgressions, and their peers will avoid socializing with them.

It's certainly reasonable for first-grade teachers to expect students to have internalized the strictures about honesty and for them to expect students to be able to differentiate right from wrong in most situations. Teachers expect students to know that they aren't permitted to take food from another child's lunchbox or to take another child's pencils or ruler. The same basic constraints, of course, also exist at home. Parents expect a six-year-old to realize that he can't appropriate his father's camera or his mother's garage-door opener simply because he wants to play with these objects. The first or second offense may be treated leniently. Subsequent offenses will elicit a stern reprimand or punishment. Further transgressions are likely to produce more severe penalties.

A child's peers have parallel expectations about respecting the conventions of property ownership. Appropriating another child's possessions is certain to trigger upset, distrust, and rejection. If the behavior is chronic, it is likely to lead to increasingly problematic social alienation.

Teachers who have students in their class who steal are faced with a formidable dilemma. Stealing not only violates the rules, but if left unchecked, the misconduct could become habitual and cause serious difficulties for children—not only in school, but also in the world beyond the classroom. Taking a toy from a store without paying for it or rummaging through someone's purse are serious offenses that are certain to result in severe penalties. If the misbehavior is not addressed and rectified, it could ultimately cause the child to become entangled in the juvenile justice system.

The rules about stealing are unmistakably clear in all venues of society, and children who do not assimilate these rules are at grave risk. The starting point in the assimilation process is for children to recognize unequivocally that it's not permissible for them to take other people's property, period. They must realize that they cannot rifle through another student's desk. They cannot take another student's lunch money, trading cards, library book, or baseball glove. They cannot take home the erasers or scissors supplied in class without permission. Breaking these rules is guaranteed to elicit their teacher's displeasure, and, if the behavior persists, it could result in an unpleasant visit to the vice principal's office, a call home, or even suspension from school. Ideally, the very thought of these consequences will be sufficient to deter any inclination to steal, but for some children even the prospect of severe consequences may not be enough.

COMMON EXPLANATIONS FOR STEALING

- Insufficient emphasis on morals and values at home
- Inadequate age-appropriate impulse control and inhibition
- Negative social influences that encourage dishonesty
- Poorly developed sense of right and wrong
- Inability to delay immediate gratification
- Underlying psychological factors that drive unacceptable behavior

The inculcation and reinforcement of a range of basic social conventions begins on the first day of school. Kindergarten teachers expect their students to have already internalized many of the do's and don'ts and to be able to differentiate right from wrong in most classroom and playground situations. Reminders may be necessary, but the rules are explicit. Students cannot hit other children with impunity. They must share kickballs, monkey bars, and climbing equipment. They must follow clearly expressed rules of decorum in the classroom, during recess, in the library, and during assemblies. As children progress into first and second grade, the rules for acceptable and unacceptable conduct are expanded, and teachers systematically reinforce these rules until they're fully assimilated and the predictable consequences for transgressions are fully appreciated.

When stealing persists despite clearly defined and consistently applied rules, appropriate reprimands, and incrementally more severe punishments, teachers must apprise the child's parents of the situation. Because this behavior most likely also occurs at home, the alert will probably not be an eye-opener for parents. The vice principal, school psychologist, or school counselor should also be informed. In an ideal world, timely intervention by a mental health professional (e.g., a licensed social worker or psychologist) would be initiated. Unfortunately, this intervention is often not provided in many school districts because of limited resources being allocated for mental health services. In reality, children in well-funded school districts are more likely to receive counseling than those in less affluent districts. The consequence of this failure to provide mental health services can be momentous. Without intervention, the wayward child could become an inveterate thief who is at risk for ending up in prison.

AN ALTERNATIVE TO THE TRADITIONAL ADULT RESPONSES TO STEALING

The common remedy for dealing with stealing is firm intervention that usually involves lectures, reprimands, and punishment. Parents and teachers have resorted to these classic interventions as behavior modification tools since time immemorial. For complex and often perplexing reasons, some children do not respond as anticipated, and the detrimental conduct persists.

This unit provides you with a procedure for addressing the issue of stealing and for helping students understand the underlying feelings that impel the behavior. The methodology incorporates the principles of cognitive behavioral change (see pages xi–xii) and is designed to help children better understand why stealing is not permitted. By means of discussion and paper-and-pencil activities, socially unacceptable behavior is negatively reinforced and socially acceptable behavior is positively reinforced. Your students are guided to two critically important insights:

- They have choices about how to behave.
- The rewards for making good choices are superior to those derived from making bad choices.

As is the case with all of the units in this program, you may elect to read the story to your students, or you may elect to have students read the story aloud. Because this is a longer anecdote, you may want to break the unit into two or more sessions and insert stopping points so that you can discuss the specific issues that arise. For example, you might ask your students, "Why do you think he said that to his mother? How do you think he felt about what was happening?" Or you might stop reading the story and say, "What do you think might happen next?" Encourage students to express their feeling and opinions, and, when appropriate, suggest alternative ways of looking at a particular issue.

Because young students generally have a relatively limited attention span, it's recommended that you keep the discussions short, unless, of course, the discussions develop their own momentum, and students want to continue talking. At any point, you may have children use the brainstorming tree (see page 12). It's important, however, to be realistic. Don't expect an immediate transformation in attitudes or behavior. Additional practice and encouragement may be needed.

If you have a student in your class who steals, it's crucial that you and your students not allude in any way to this child during the class discussion. To do so would be humiliating and traumatizing. Before beginning to read the story, you might say, "We're only dealing with the child who is described in the story. We're not discussing any students in this class or in this school." If other students attempt to make references to a specific child, you should immediately stop them by repeating the preceding admonition.

The anecdote is designed to help the student who steals better understand and ideally modify behavior that could create major problems now and down the road. The student-oriented activities and exercises provide you with a template for becoming an effective mentor in dealing with the issue.

The story is intended to serve as a catalyst for a discussion and examination of the issues. To reiterate a key point that was made in the Introduction, the goal is not to transform you into an "instant psychologist" but, rather, to show you how to apply your teaching skills and insights. The operating premise is straightforward—namely, that empathetic and attuned frontline educators can help students acquire important insights that will equip them to deal with challenges and dilemmas and help them handle situations that might otherwise overwhelm them.

EXAMINING THE STORY

The description of the protagonist's behavior should resonate in students who are stealing. Most children realize when they're breaking the rules. Of course, those who chronically break the rules may be in denial about their transgressions or may delude themselves that what they're doing is OK. (*Please note:* To make the following examination of the issues more concrete, you may want to skip ahead and read the story on page 68.)

The anecdote describes a child who is forced to deal with the unpleasant consequences of stealing. At the same time, the story delivers a positive message: Children can learn from their mistakes and avoid repeating them. The key point you want your students to grasp is that they have choices about how they behave.

The anecdote and questions that follow provide an opportunity for your students to consider the factors that may cause children to steal. The story also explores the likely repercussions when a child takes another's possessions and examines how Zachary's father deals with the issue. By helping students understand another child's maladaptive conduct and by encouraging them to consider how to alter this unacceptable behavior, you're clearly affirming that problems are fixable and that practical solutions for dealing with predicaments and temptations can be devised.

As is the case in all of the units in this program, Zachary's story isn't exclusively directed at children who are stealing. It's also aimed at youngsters who may be affected by another student's misconduct. Certainly, anger is the common visceral reaction of children whose possessions are stolen. No one appreciates being victimized. By helping your students better understand the feelings and thoughts of a child who steals, you're certainly not encouraging children to condone the behavior. Rather, you're making them more aware of some of the underlying issues, and you're showing them how they can actively participate in the process of reorienting the unacceptable conduct.

THE QUESTIONS THAT FOLLOW THE STORY

See page 10 for suggestions about how to present the questions that help students carefully examine the story and understand the key issues. The procedural template is essentially the same in every unit in this program.

For Students

The Child Who Steals

THE STORY

1   Zachary hadn't fallen asleep yet. His bedroom door
2 was partially open, and he could hear his parents talking
3 in the living room.

4   "Do you know where my little flashlight is?" Zachary's
5 dad asked.

6   "I haven't seen it," Zachary's mother answered.

7   "I know it was in the drawer near the bed. I remember
8 seeing it two nights ago."

9   After a few minutes, Zachary's dad walked quietly into
10 Zachary's bedroom. The eight-year-old pretended to be
11 asleep. Although his eyes were mostly closed, he could
12 still see his dad looking down at him because of the light
13 coming in from the hallway. Zachary didn't move a muscle,
14 and his father didn't say anything. Then he turned around
15 and left the room, quietly closing the door behind him.

16   Zachary listened very hard for a few moments, but
17 he could no longer hear his mother and father talking.
18 Reaching under the covers, he turned on the tiny flash-
19 light that he had placed next to his leg, and he scooted his
20 head under the blankets. Zachary could see himself in the
21 light. He moved his fingers and watched the shadows they
22 made on the inside of the covers. He pretended the finger
23 shadows were ghosts in a cave. Then Zachary pushed his
24 head up from under the covers to see if he could see the
25 light from the flashlight through the blankets. Satisfied that

Zachary pretends to be sleeping.

26 he couldn't, he stuck his head under the blankets, and he
27 began playing with the flashlight again. He turned it on
28 and off. He pointed it at his toes to see if he could make
29 toe shadows. He placed his hand over the light, and his
30 hand became red. He could actually see the bones in his
31 fingers. Then he put the flashlight inside of his blue
32 pajama top. The light became blue, and the cave under
33 the blankets also became blue.

34 "This is fun," Zachary thought. After a few minutes, he
35 got tired of playing. Feeling very sleepy, he switched off
36 the flashlight and left it under the covers next to his leg. In
37 the morning, he planned to put it in his secret hiding
38 place. Before he knew it, he was asleep, and when he
39 opened his eyes, it was morning. His mother was gently
40 shaking him to wake up for school.

41 Zachary went to the bathroom to wash his hands
42 and face and brush his teeth. While he was brushing his
43 teeth, his father came into the bathroom. He was already
44 dressed for work. He kissed Zachary and said, "Good
45 morning! How'd you sleep?" He always asked the same
46 question every morning. Zachary replied, "Good."

47 "By the way, did you happen to see the little flashlight that
48 I keep in the top drawer of my nightstand?" his father asked.

49 Zachary kept on brushing his teeth. After he spit out
50 the toothpaste and rinsed out his mouth, he answered,

Zachary shining the flashlight under the covers.

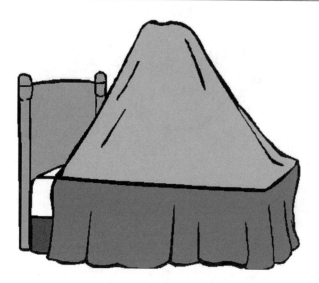

51 "No." He didn't look at his dad. When he glanced at the
52 mirror, he could see his father looking at him.

53 "Are you sure?" his father asked with a very serious tone.

54 "Yes," Zachary answered in a soft voice.

55 "It's strange," his father replied. "I have no idea where it is."

56 His father's voice didn't sound very convincing, but he
57 didn't say anything more about the flashlight. He kissed
58 Zachary good-bye and left for work.

59 Because he was running late for school, Zachary
60 rushed to get his books and papers and stuff them in his
61 backpack. He grabbed his lunch bag, kissed his mother
62 good-bye, and raced out the door. He could see the
63 school bus turning the corner two blocks away. If he ran
64 hard, he had just enough time to make it to the bus stop.

65 Zachary was the last child to get into the bus. As he set-
66 tled into his seat, a terrible thought flashed through his
67 mind. His eyes went wide, and his heart started to beat. He
68 remembered that he had left the flashlight under the covers
69 and had forgotten to put it in his secret hiding place. If his
70 mom went into his room to fix the covers on his bed, she'd
71 find it! Zachary hoped that she was running late for work
72 and that she wouldn't go into his room.

73 74 75 When the bus arrived at school, the children rushed to the playground to play before the bell rang. Zachary saw his friend Joshua, and the two boys started playing tag.

76 77 78 79 80 When the bell rang, the boys lined up with the other children. Joshua showed Zachary a new plastic action figure his mom bought him. The toy was about six inches high and all gold. By twisting it, you could transform the rocket ship into an alien monster.

81 82 "This is really neat!" Zachary exclaimed. "I'm going to ask my mom to buy me one."

83 84 85 86 During class, Zachary had difficulty with some math problems. Mrs. Saxon walked over to his desk and explained how to do the problems. When it was time for recess, Zachary still had three problems to do.

87 88 89 "Zachary, I want you to finish these problems before you go to recess," Mrs. Saxon said. "You can come out to the playground when you've finished."

90 91 92 Zachary was angry because he wanted to go out and play. But he knew he could finish the problems quickly if he worked hard.

93 94 95 96 97 98 99 100 101 102 103 When Zachary was done, he put his paper on Mrs. Saxon's desk. As he walked out the door, he passed by Joshua's desk. Joshua's unzipped backpack was behind his chair. Zachary could see the action figure near the top. Kneeling down, he picked up the toy. He twisted the rocket ship, and it became an alien monster. Zachary loved the shiny gold color, and he very badly wanted one just like it. It wasn't fair to have to wait until his mother bought him one. And besides, he wasn't even sure that she would get it for him right away. She might say that he'd have to wait until his birthday, and that was three months away.

104 105 106 107 108 109 Looking around to make sure no one else was in the room, Zachary quickly put the toy in his pocket. He walked back to his desk and stuffed the Transformer into the bottom of his own backpack. He covered the toy with papers and books and zipped the bag. He then hurriedly went out the door and rushed down the hall to the playground.

Zachary looking in Joshua's book bag.

110 Joshua discovered that his action figure was missing
111 when he came back from recess.

112 Zachary could see him searching for it in his bag.
113 Joshua didn't say anything to Mrs. Saxon about the miss-
114 ing toy. He knew he wasn't allowed to bring toys to school,
115 and he had already gotten into trouble for doing so.

116 When the lunch bell rang, Zachary stood next to Joshua
117 as they lined up. The two boys walked together to the lunch-
118 room. Zachary could tell that his friend was very upset.

119 "I can't find my Transformer," Joshua said. "I know it was
120 in my backpack when I went to recess. Someone must have
121 taken it." Joshua was almost about to cry. Zachary pre-
122 tended that he didn't know about the missing action figure.

123 "Maybe it dropped out of your bag and maybe some-
124 one picked it up," Zachary suggested. He didn't think that
125 he was lying because Joshua hadn't asked him if he had
126 taken the toy.

127 "If my mom finds out I took the toy to school, she'll be
128 mad. And if I tell her I lost it, she'll also be mad. I don't
129 know what to do," Joshua said sadly.

130 "I think it would be better not to tell her,"
131 Zachary said. "When my mom buys me one, I'll lend it to

132
133 you so you can show your mom that you still have it," Zachary suggested helpfully.

134
135 "When do you think your mom will buy you one?" Joshua asked.

136 "Maybe tomorrow."

137
138
139 Zachary decided to return Joshua's toy after his mom bought him one. He would play with it for now and then tell his friend that he found his Transformer in the bushes.

140
141 When Zachary returned home from school, his mom was waiting for him. He had forgotten about the flashlight!

142
143
144 "Zachary, I discovered your father's flashlight in your bed when I went to straighten the covers. How did it get there?" she asked sternly.

145
146 "I found it on the floor," he answered, feeling guilty about not telling the truth.

147
148
149 "Well, when your dad gets home, you can explain to him how the flashlight ended up in your bed," his mom said in a stern voice.

150
151
152
153 Zachary could tell that his mother didn't believe him. He was sure that his father would make him tell the truth. He was also sure that he would be punished for taking the flashlight without permission.

154
155
156
157
158
159 Zachary heard his father come home while he was in his room doing his homework. It was 6:00. He could barely hear his parents talking in the kitchen, but he was sure they were talking about the flashlight. Then his mother called him to come down for dinner. Zachary was very nervous as he walked to the kitchen.

160
161 "Hi, Zack," his father said when Zachary came into the kitchen.

162
163
164
165 Zachary's dad didn't say anything about the flashlight during dinner. Zachary concentrated on eating his chicken, salad, and baked potato. His father asked him how things went in school. Zachary replied, "Good." He

166
167
168
169
170
didn't really want to talk about school. Zachary could barely eat because he was worried what his dad would say after dinner. He knew he was in trouble and would be punished. It was horrible having to wait for something bad to happen.

171
172
173
When dinner was over, Zachary's dad said, "We need to talk, Zachary. Let's go into the living room." His father was carrying a paper bag.

174
175
176
Zachary's father asked him to sit on the couch. He sat in a big armchair facing Zachary. He had the paper bag in his lap.

177
178
179
180
"Your mother told me that she found my flashlight in your bed. Did you take it from my drawer? Before you answer, I want you to make sure that you tell me the truth," his father said.

181
182
183
184
185
186
187
Zachary was tempted to say he didn't know how the flashlight got into his bed, but he knew his father wouldn't believe him. Zachary knew that he wouldn't be able to explain how the flashlight ended up in his bed. If he said that he found it on the floor or in the kitchen, he'd have to tell more lies, and everything would get worse. He decided to tell the truth.

188
189
"I took it," he said in a very low voice, as he stared at the floor.

190
191
"I see," his father said. "Do you know what I have in this paper bag, Zachary?"

192
"No."

193
194
195
196
197
198
"Your mother was vacuuming your room. She moved your bed and found a small box. She was curious and looked inside. These are the things that she found in the box." Zachary's father spilled out the contents of the bag onto the coffee table. The stuff had come from his secret hiding place.

199
200
201
202
"Here's the small binoculars that I couldn't find last month. Here's the pedometer that I use to figure out how far I walk. I thought I had misplaced it. And here is my magnifying glass."

203   When Zachary saw the things he had taken spread out
204 on the coffee table, tears started to roll down his cheeks.
205 His dad knew about everything!

206   "Your mom got a call from Joshua's mother. She said
207 that a toy that Joshua brought to school is missing. It was
208 in his backpack when he went to recess, but it was gone
209 when he came back from recess. You played with the toy
210 before school, and you told Joshua that you wanted one
211 just like it. You were also the only child in the classroom
212 during recess," his father said in a very serious voice.

213   Zachary was crying softly, and he couldn't look at his
214 father.

215   "Did you take Joshua's toy?" Zachary's father continued.

216   "Yes," Zachary replied in a very tiny voice.

217   "I want you to go to your room and get it," his father
218 said.

219   Zachary got up from the sofa and went to get the toy.
220 He had hidden it under his mattress. Zachary felt like run-
221 ning away and never coming home. When he returned to
222 the living room, he put the Transformer on the coffee table
223 and sat down on the couch. Zachary's father placed the
224 toy, flashlight, binoculars, pedometer, and magnifying
225 glass next to each other.

226   "After we are done talking, I want you to call Joshua and
227 tell him that you have his toy. We'll drive to his house. You
228 will give the toy back to him and apologize for taking it."

229   "Could you do it for me?" Zachary asked glumly.

230   "No, son. You took the toy, and you'll have to return it
231 yourself."

232   Zachary was staring at the floor. He was still too
233 embarrassed to look at his father.

234   "Now, we have to deal with what happened at home,"
235 his father continued. "You took my things without asking
236 permission. You didn't have to do this. You could have
237 asked me to use them. And do you know what?"

238   "What?" Zachary asked timidly.

239   "I would have let you borrow them if you had asked
240 permission and agreed to put them back. Then I would
241 know where my things are, and you'd be responsible for
242 taking care of them. Do you understand?"

243   "Yes," Zachary replied.

244   "Tell me in your own words what I just told you," his
245 father said.

246   "If I ask you, I can borrow your stuff."

247   "Well, you could ask to borrow something, and I would
248 then decide if I wanted to let you play with it. Do you
249 understand?"

250   "Yes," Zachary replied.

251   "OK. Let's practice the system. What things on this
252 table would you like to borrow?"

253   "I'd like to borrow the binoculars," Zachary replied in a
254 low voice.

255   "All right, I'll let you borrow them. We'll make a list of
256 the things you would like to borrow and write them on this
257 piece of paper. I am going to write 'Borrowing List' at the
258 top of the paper and binoculars on the first line." His father
259 called out each letter as he wrote it. "B-i-n-o-c-u-l-a-r-s. I'll
260 write today's date on the same line, and you'll put a check
261 after the date. This means that you're borrowing the binoc-
262 ulars today and that you're responsible for them. When
263 you return the binoculars you'll draw a line through the
264 checkmark. I'll empty a drawer in the kitchen where you
265 can put the things you return. We'll attach the borrowing
266 list to the refrigerator door with a magnet. You'll check the
267 things you borrow 'in' and 'out' just like you do in the
268 library. Do you understand the system?" his father asked.

269   "Yes," Zachary replied. Zachary's father pushed the
270 binoculars over to Zachary's side of the coffee table.

271   "Now ask me what else you would like to borrow."

272   "I'd like to borrow the pedometer, the flashlight, and the
273   magnifying glass," Zachary replied.

274   "We'll add them to the list. I have another flashlight
275   that I can put in my nightstand drawer in case there's an
276   emergency. This flashlight must always remain there.
277   Understood?"

278   "Yes," Zachary answered.

279   "Now, we still have one more thing to discuss, Zachary.
280   Do you know what it is?"

281   "No," Zachary answered.

282   "We need to discuss the punishment for taking my
283   things and Joshua's toy."

284   Zachary didn't say anything. He had forgotten about
285   the punishment.

286   "Your mother and I have decided that you can't watch
287   TV or use your bicycle for one week. If you take things that
288   don't belong to you again without permission, the next
289   punishment will be worse. Is this clear, Zachary?"

290   "Yes," Zachary replied in a very soft voice.

291   "Tell me what I just said in your own words."

292   "I'll get in big trouble if I take other people's things
293   again without permission."

294   "Correct."

295   "It's time to drive to Joshua's house. I want you to call
296   Joshua and tell him that we're on our way over to his
297   house with his toy."

298   Zachary's father dialed the number, and when
299   Joshua's mother answered, he asked if Zachary could talk
300   to Joshua. Then he handed the phone to Zachary.

Zachary's father dialing Joshua's telephone number.

301   "Hello," Joshua said when he got on the phone.

302   "Hi. It's me. I took your toy. My dad is driving me over
303   to your house now, and I'll give it back to you."

304   "OK," Joshua said.

305   During the drive to Joshua's house, Zachary and his
306   father didn't speak for a few minutes. Zachary looked out
307   the window and was thinking about what he would say to
308   Joshua.

309   "I know that this is embarrassing for you, Zachary, but
310   it's an important lesson. We must take responsibility for
311   our actions," his father said. "What do you think it means
312   to take responsibility for our actions?"

313   "If we do something bad, we have to be punished,"
314   Zachary answered.

315   "It's more than that. We make choices, and there are
316   often consequences for these choices. For example, if you
317   tell lies to your friends, the consequence is that your
318   friends won't believe you. If you steal from your friends,
319   the consequence is that your friends won't trust you. You

320 must take responsibility for the consequences, the good
321 ones and the bad ones."

322 The car pulled up in front of Joshua's house, and
323 Zachary and his dad walked to the front door. Zachary's
324 dad pressed the bell, and Joshua's mother let them in.

325 When Joshua came into the living room, Zachary
326 was very embarrassed, and he couldn't say anything.
327 Realizing this, his father helped him get started.

328 "Joshua, Zachary has something he wants to tell you. Go
329 ahead, Zachary," his father said in a firm but gentle voice.

330 "Joshua, I'm sorry that I took your Transformer,"
331 Zachary said.

332 He handed Joshua the toy. Zachary didn't know what
333 else to say. He just stared at the floor and wondered if
334 Joshua would still want to be his friend.

335 "We have to go home now," Zachary's father said.
336 "Zachary still has homework to do."

337 Zachary was surprised when Joshua waved good-bye.
338 Maybe his friend would forgive him after all.

339 When they were back in the car, Zachary's dad put his
340 hand gently on his son's head. He smiled warmly.

341 "I liked the way you handled that, Zachary. I'm proud of
342 you."

343 Zachary couldn't believe his ears.

344 "Even though I took Joshua's toy and your things?"

345 "You made mistakes, and you paid the price for your
346 mistakes. When you learn from mistakes, you acquire
347 good judgment. Taking things without permission is wrong.
348 I have faith in you, and I know that you won't do it again."

349 Zachary didn't say anything on the way home. What a
350 day it had been. One thing was for sure—he was done
351 stealing.

ORAL QUESTIONS

■ Why do you think that Zachary took his father's things without permission?

Function: *Developing analytical and critical thinking skills.*

Comments: The types of responses you're looking for include:*

- He wanted to play with the things so badly that he couldn't stop himself from taking them.
- He thought it would be fun to play with the things.
- He didn't think his dad would mind.
- He thought his dad would not let him borrow the things if he asked him.
- He didn't think his dad would find out that he took his things.
- He planned on returning them before he got into trouble.
- He decided not to think about what the consequences would be.

*You don't need to elicit all of these reasons. Be prepared for off-target or illogical responses, which should be treated with sensitivity. As students participate in these class discussions, their reasoning and analytical thinking skills will improve. You want to create a safe context in which students can freely express their ideas and feelings.

■ What words would you use to describe Zachary? Explain why you've chosen these words.

Function: *Developing observational skills, perceptiveness, and empathy.*

Comments: The types of responses you're looking for include:

- Not smart.
- Willing to take risks.
- Unafraid of consequences.
- Dishonest.
- Tells lies.

■ Why do you think Zachary lied to his mom and dad about the flashlight?

Function: *Developing analytical thinking skills.*

Comments: The types of responses you're looking for include:

- He was afraid he would get into trouble and be punished.
- He thought he could get away with taking the flashlight.
- It was easier to lie than to tell the truth.
- He lied without thinking about the consequences.
- He was in the habit of lying.

■ How do you think Joshua felt after he realized that Zachary had taken his new toy?

Function: *Developing analytical and critical thinking skills, insight, and empathy.*

Comments: The types of responses you're looking for include:

- He felt angry.
- He felt sad.
- He felt hurt.
- He felt upset.
- He felt confused about why Zachary would take his toy.
- He felt that his friend had let him down.
- He felt like he didn't want to be friends with Zachary.
- He felt that he couldn't trust Zachary any more.

NOTE: At this juncture, you may want to introduce and help your students understand the concepts of feeling *betrayed* and *disillusioned.*

■ Do you have any ideas about how Zachary's dad might have handled the problem differently when he discovered that Zachary had taken his things and Joshua's toy?

Function: *Learning to brainstorm and problem solve. (It's recommended that you use the brainstorming tree on page 12 with students.)*

Comments: The types of responses you are looking for include:

- He could have punished Zachary more severely.
- He could have forbidden him to borrow any of his things.
- He could have gotten very mad and yelled at Zachary.
- He could have forbidden him from having playdates with friends for two weeks.
- He could have taken away all of Zachary's toys.

■ Why do you think that Zachary's dad insisted on driving to Joshua's house so that Zachary could return the toy?

Function: *Developing analytical and critical thinking skills and insight.*

Comments: The types of responses you are looking for include:

- He wanted Zachary to apologize personally for taking the toy.
- He wanted to teach Zachary a lesson about stealing that he would remember.
- He wanted to have Zachary take responsibility for what he had done.

- He wanted Zachary to recognize the consequences.
- He wanted Zachary to handle the problem himself, even if he was embarrassed.

■ Why do you think children take things that don't belong to them?

Function: *Enhancing analytical and critical thinking skills.*

Comments: The types of responses you are looking for include:

- They want something very badly and want to have it right away.
- They can't control themselves when they want something.
- They don't care if they make other people unhappy when they steal.
- They may be poor and know that their parents won't buy them what they want.
- Their parents may not have taught them that stealing is wrong.
- They may believe that they can get away with taking other people's things.
- They may not care about the punishments.

■ Could you give examples of temptations that some children might find hard to resist?

Function: *Developing analytical thinking skills.*

Comments: The types of responses you are looking for include:

- Keeping money that you find on the sidewalk.
- Taking a piece of candy in a supermarket.
- Cheating on a test.
- Not telling the truth if you know the truth might get you into trouble.
- Cheating when playing a game.

■ What could a child do to not give in to these temptations?

Function: *Developing analytical thinking skills and heightened awareness and insight.*

Comments: The types of responses you are looking for include:

- He could remind himself that stealing, cheating, and lying are wrong.
- He could remind himself that he should act in ways that make him proud of himself.
- He could think about the consequences if he cheats, steals, or lies.
- He could remind himself that his parents would be very sad if he did something wrong.

■ Why would a child's parents be concerned if their child is dishonest?

Function: *Developing analytical, evaluative, and expressive language skills.*

Comments: The types of responses you are looking for include:

- They would be concerned that their child would get into trouble.
- They would be concerned that their child might steal from a store and be taken to jail.
- They would be concerned that their child would lose his friends.
- They would be embarrassed by their child's behavior.
- They would be concerned that others would consider them to be bad parents.
- They would be concerned that their child might become a thief when he's an adult and end up in prison.

■ What are the consequences of being dishonest?

Function: *Developing analytical, evaluative, and critical thinking skills.*

Comments: The types of responses you are looking for include:

- Losing your friends.
- Making your parents angry.
- Making your teachers angry.
- Getting into trouble.
- Being punished.
- Not being trusted.

■ If Zachary were your friend, is there anything you could do to help him?

Function: *Developing analytical, strategic, critical thinking, and problem-solving skills.*

Comments: The types of responses you are looking for include:

- I could tell him that it's wrong to steal.
- I could tell him to talk to me before he's tempted to steal something.
- I could offer to let him borrow some of my things.
- I could tell him that I wouldn't be his friend if he takes things that don't belong to him.
- I could tell him that I'd tell the teacher if I see him steal in school.
- I could tell him that I'd tell his mom if I see him steal outside of school.

OPTIONAL ACTIVITY: CAREFUL READING AND ANALYSIS OF THE STORY

(These exercises are designed for students who can read at the second-grade level and above.)

- While Zachary was in the bathroom brushing his teeth, his father asked him two questions about his missing flashlight. Zachary answered both of the questions with lies. Go back and find the questions that Zachary's father asked and underline them one time. Then underline the two lies Zachary told twice. (Hint: You can find the questions and lies in lines 47 to 54.)
- When Zachary was first talking with Joshua about the missing toy, he suggested what might have happened to the toy. This suggestion was actually a type of lie because Zachary really knew that he was the child who had actually taken the toy. Underline the sentence in which Zachary misleads his friend. (Hint: You can find this sentence in lines 123 to 126.)
- Zachary decided to return the toy after his mother bought one for him. He planned to tell Joshua a lie to explain why he had the toy. Underline the sentence that describes the lie Zachary was planning to tell Joshua. (Hint: You can find the sentences in lines 137 to 139.)
- Find and underline the sentences in the story that describe the "library type checkout system" that Zachary's dad wanted Zachary to use when he had permission to borrow something. Number each part of the system. (Hint: You can find the description of the system in lines 255 to 268.)
- Find and underline the sentence that describes the punishment that Zachary received for taking things that didn't belong to him. (Hint: You can find the sentence in lines 286 to 289.)
- Zachary and his father discussed the consequences for certain behaviors as they drove to Joshua's to return the toy. Find and underline the two examples of consequences that Zachary's father described. (Hint: You can find the sentences in lines 316 to 319.)
- Find and underline the sentence that describes what Zachary decides about stealing. (Hint: You can find the sentence in lines 350 to 351.)

SUPPLEMENTAL REPRODUCIBLE EXERCISES

(These reinforcement exercises can be completed in class or assigned for homework.)

❑ **If you feel tempted to take something that isn't yours, what could you do to stop yourself from stealing? Write your ideas in the space below.**

1. _____

2. _____

3. _____

4. _____

❏ **Rate Zachary's father's decision to make Zachary go to Joshua's house to return the toy he took.**

Using a Scale

If you've forgotten how to use a scale to rate something, look back on page 25.

Choose the number that best describes what you think about the idea of Zachary going to Joshua's house and returning the toy to him.

1	2	3	4	5	6	7	8	9	10
Poor				Average					Excellent

❏ **Why did you choose the number that you circled?**

_____

_____

_____

_____

❏ **Zachary was surprised when Joshua waved good-bye to him. Do you think that Joshua still wanted to be Zachary's friend? Yes No**

If you answered "yes," explain your reasons in the space below.

_____

_____

_____

If you answered "no," explain your reasons in the space below.

_____

_____

_____

❑ **If you saw a child in your class stealing, what could you do about it?**

1. _____

2. _____

3. _____

❑ **If you saw someone stealing and you told your parents, the other child's parents, or your teacher, how would this make you feel?**

1. _____

2. _____

3. _____

❑ **List the reasons a child might feel guilty for doing the right thing.**

1. _____

2. _____

3. _____

❑ **Would you feel guilty about reporting that a child has stolen something?   Yes   No**

If you answered "yes," explain your reasons for feeling guilty in the space below.

_____

_____

_____

If you answered "no," explain your reasons for not feeling guilty in the space below.

_____

_____

_____

❑ **List some reasons why a punishment for doing something wrong might be good for the child.**

1. _____

2. _____

3. _____

❑ **Would you be willing to be friends with a child who steals from you? Yes   No**

If you answered "yes," explain your reasons in the space below.

_____

_____

_____

If you answered "no," explain your reasons in the space below.

_____

_____

_____

FOLLOW-UP AND APPLICATION

Despite having extensively examined the issue of stealing with your class, you may not necessarily see immediate behavioral changes in children who are prone to stealing. Negative conduct patterns can be difficult to break, and some youngsters may persist in taking things that do not belong to them.

Follow-up and reinforcement are critical components in the equation that produces meaningful behavioral changes. In a nonpreachy way, you should remind students of what it means to be honest. Students who steal must also be privately alerted when you become aware of their misconduct. Be prepared, of course, for excuses, denials, and blaming. For this reason, it's important to have personally seen the misdeed or, if possible, to have corroboration if another child reports the stealing. As a general rule, the child reporting the stealing is probably telling the truth.

Students must be repeatedly reminded that there are not-to-be-broken rules of conduct and that there are consequences for breaking these rules. The consequences might include missing recess, a conference with the child's parents, or if there continue to be repeated incidences of stealing, a trip to the vice principal's office.

At the same time, you must privately affirm children who are making positive changes in their behavior. You must let them know that you're aware of the fact that they are no longing taking things that do not belong to them and that you're pleased and proud of them.

CONCRETE REINFORCEMENTS

You might have students break up into small groups and have each group create a poster about the school rules regarding taking other children's possessions. These posters, which will serve as tangible reminders of the issues examined in the unit, might also spell out the consequences for breaking the rules. You could then affix the posters to a wall and periodically have the entire class read in unison one or more of the posters aloud. This reinforcement is a critically important component in the cognitive behavior change model described in the Introduction (see page xii).

Students who are guided to a better understanding of why certain conduct is not acceptable are more likely to alter maladaptive behaviors. They must also be helped to recognize the impact of their conduct on others and furnished with repeated opportunities to practice acting more appropriately. Providing acknowledgment and praise for genuine improvement is an essential element in the reorientation process. The acknowledgment and praise for not stealing, however, should obviously be delivered in private, because you certainly don't want to embarrass the child who has a history of stealing.

Another means for reinforcing positive change is to have students create skits that recap what they've discussed in class. For example, children could write a skit in which a child (not a student who has actually been stealing!) might open another student's desk, look around furtively, take something, and put it in his backpack. Other students might enter the room and witness what's happening. They might shake their heads disapprovingly and inform the teacher about the transgression. The child playing the role of the teacher might point to the door and send the child to the vice principal's office. The child playing the role of the vice principal might look very stern and pretend to call the child's parents on the phone. When the parents arrive in her office, they, too, would look very stern and distressed, and they would inform their child about the punishments that will result.

Enhancing students' awareness of the rules and the consequences for breaking the rules is a critically important step in preparing children to deal with society's covenants. This procedure can play a vital role in preventing children from ultimately becoming enmeshed in the criminal justice system. Teaching children not to steal is an unequivocally attainable goal, if the reorientation process begins early enough and if the cognitive behavioral change procedures are fundamentally sound and consistently applied. Strengthening students' awareness of socially acceptable values, societal strictures, and cause-and-effect principles is also an unequivocally attainable goal. With effective instruction and mentoring, you can systematically enhance your students' analytical, strategic thinking, and problem-solving skills, and you can affirm critically important values such as honesty, integrity, and truthfulness. The impact of this guidance on your students' lives will be profound and lasting.

Unit 4

The Child
Who Tells Lies

For Educators

Examining the Dynamics and Implications of Lying

The factors that cause children to steal (see Unit 3) are also relevant to understanding why children lie. As previously stated, children's maladaptive behavior offers a portal into the underlying emotions that drive their conduct.

Occasional untruthfulness and "white lies" must be differentiated from chronic lying. Although the extent and regularity of a child's lying has a bearing on the urgency for intervention, any lying by children represents unacceptable conduct that must be firmly discouraged. Certainly, chronic lying is more problematic than sporadic lying, but even intermittent untruthfulness is worrisome, and the behavior needs to be addressed and remedied.

Recurring falsehoods are a red flag signaling a proclivity that could produce serious negative consequences for children not only in school, but also in the world beyond the classroom. Unless this conduct is reoriented, lying could become an ingrained habit that is certain to create major problems for children as they proceed through life.

One need only observe preschoolers to recognize that telling fibs and expedient falsehoods is common during the early stages of development when children often deny their transgressions or blame others to escape censure. The conventions about honesty and truthfulness are still in the process of being assimilated. By the time children enter kindergarten, however, they should know that lying is wrong and unacceptable. Yes, some may still occasionally succumb to the tempting expediency of lying, but their recognition and adherence to the basic social conventions regarding truthfulness should be fairly well established, and by this juncture, they should realize that lying is not permitted at home or in school. They should also realize that there are predictable consequences for breaking this rule.

As is the case with stealing, the traditional explanations for lying typically focus on parental shortcomings. The behavior is usually attributed to inadequate teaching, modeling, enforcement, and reinforcement at home of core values and rules about being honest and truthful. This explanation may be accurate, but it may also be overly simplistic. There may, in fact, be other plausible explanations that include the following:

- Poor impulse control
- Poor self-esteem
- The need to impress others by exaggerating or prevaricating
- The need to evade responsibility
- The fear of punishment for transgressions

For some children, lying becomes the convenient path of least resistance when they're faced with problems, challenges, or accountability for their actions. Rather than confront and deal with difficult situations head-on, these children choose to lie and, by so doing, avoid having to come to grips with unpleasantness. Of course, there are many adults who resort to the same behavior.

TRAINING CHILDREN TO BE TRUTHFUL

During the formative years, children are continually being indoctrinated with rules, boundaries, and limits that are imparted by their parents and teachers, and they are expected to assimilate these regulations dutifully. Although a certain amount of rule testing is to be expected, some children seem impelled to challenge the limits repeatedly. For these youngsters, lying to get what they want, justify their behavior, avoid blame, or escape responsibility could become standard operating procedure unless the conduct is vigorously, consistently, and effectively discouraged. If left unchallenged, the use of expedient lies to avoid responsibility or censure (e.g., "I didn't push Joshua. He pushed me!") could quickly evolve into an engrained habit and become part of a child's comfort zone.

One of the primary objectives of parents and teachers during the formative years is to train children to think about their actions so that they aren't constantly operating on automatic pilot and acting impulsively and thoughtlessly. The extended process of heightening their awareness, enhancing their analytical thinking, and inculcating basic values is a requisite to helping youngsters develop socially acceptable behavior and critical intelligence.

As previously noted, the capacity to self-regulate is not fully developed in young children. Some youngsters misbehave and then prevaricate to avoid having to deal with the consequences. Others, and especially those who are insecure, lie or exaggerate to impress their peers, parents, or teachers. Children resorting to this behavior may convince themselves that their lies are actually true. This unconscious need to self-delude and self-deceive, of course, can also be observed in adults. TV interviews with convicted felons underscore the phenomenon. A prisoner stares into the camera and states with total aplomb that he is completely innocent despite the irrefutable evidence that unequivocally confirms his guilt.

Examples of children lying to protect themselves from the repercussions of their actions abound. A three-year-old may tell his mother that he didn't break the lamp in the living room even though he's standing right next to the broken lamp. A four-year-old may deny that she took her mother's earring from the jewelry box even though her mother discovered the earring under the child's pillow. A five-year-old may deny that he intentionally pushed another child to the ground even though the teacher saw him do so, and a six-year-old may deny that she tore a poster on the wall even though eyewitnesses attest to the transgression. In each of these instances, lying functions to protect the child from disapprobation and to deflect accountability.

EXPANDING THE LIST OF EXPLANATIONS FOR LYING

- Insufficient instruction and reinforcement of values at home
- Inadequate impulse control
- Convenience (i.e., the path of least resistance)
- The need to avoid responsibility for one's actions
- The desire to escape the consequences for misbehavior
- Deficient self-esteem, which stimulates the need to exaggerate or prevaricate

TRADITIONAL ADULT RESPONSES TO LYING

Since time immemorial, parents have handled children's lying with firm reminders about the rules and with consistent negative reinforcement for transgressions. "You must tell the truth" is as common a litany during the formative years as the admonition, "You may not take another person's possessions without permission." The typical consequences for transgressions include being sent to one's room, being forbidden to watch TV, and being grounded.

Aware parents realize that they must repeatedly define and clarify the boundaries of acceptable behavior and that they must, if necessary, repeatedly exhort children to abide by these limits. This ongoing procedure of defining acceptable conduct is integral to responsible parenting. Certainly, some children "get it" quickly, and lying is not a major issue. Others require additional reinforcement, clarification, support, and admonishing before they finally assimilate the prohibitions.

The goal of limit setting is to help children develop age-appropriate inhibition, a requisite to effective social functioning. Parents must train their child to recognize and resist self-damaging impulses, and they must condition their child to recognize and conform to the rules that define permissible behavior. A neurological phenomenon necessitates this training. Consistent impulse control is not natural in children because the prefrontal cortex of the brain that regulates impulsiveness is not yet fully developed. This explains why many children are prone to dart out into the street, take excessive risks, use poor judgment, and break rules that they've been taught to obey.

Systematic and consistent reinforcement of the codes for acceptable behavior at home and in school are clearly vital during the formative years. Externally enforced limits and predictable, consistently applied consequences for misconduct are essential until children can demonstrate that the rules have been assimilated and are being self-enforced.

One of the primary goals of this program is to help your students acquire a greater awareness of their own behavior, a better understanding of the impact of their behavior on others, a clear appreciation of predictable consequences for misconduct, and a heightened cognizance of the desirable payoffs that accrue when they think and act appropriately. These insights are central to the cognitive behavioral change instructional methodology that runs thematically through the program. (See pages xii–xiii for a description of cognitive behavioral change methodology.)

THE ROLE OF THE TEACHER

Instilling an awareness of and appreciation for core social values is clearly not an exclusive parental responsibility. The process must also be consistently reinforced in school.

Teachers in the lower grades cannot escape the necessity of acting in loco parentis (i.e., as parental stand-ins). This obligation to reinforce the basic covenants about truthfulness is driven by a harsh reality: Students who continue to lie are destined to face major problems in all venues of their lives. Teachers have an obligation to intervene proactively when they observe a pattern of lying. Simply meting out punishments for untruthfulness, however, may not be sufficient. Helping students better understand why they're lying and helping them learn how to handle challenging situations without feeling it necessary to resort to lying is clearly preferable to imposing repeated reprimands and punishments, although these negative reinforcements may certainly be appropriate in many situations.

It's reasonable for teachers to expect school-age students to understand that it's wrong to lie. It's also reasonable for teachers to expect their students to be able to resist the inclination to be untruthful for the sake of expedience. And it's equally reasonable for teachers to expect children to recognize that when they choose to lie, their behavior is certain to disappoint their parents, teachers, and peers and to elicit a strong negative reaction. Their teachers and parents will get upset, and their friends will probably reject them. That lying works at cross-purposes with having and maintaining friendships is an immutable cause-and-effect reality that all children must fathom.

EXAMINING THE STORY

Ideally, the description of the protagonist's behavior and the implications of this behavior will resonate in children who are lying. Most children recognize when they're breaking the rules and doing something wrong. Of course, children who chronically lie may be in denial. They may delude themselves that they're not lying or rationalize that it's OK to lie. (*Please note:* To make the following examination of the issues more concrete, you may want to skip ahead and read the story on page 98.)

The story describes a child who is forced to deal with the very unpleasant consequences of lying. At the same time, the story delivers a positive message, namely, that children can learn from their mistakes and avoid repeating them. As has been noted previously, the message that you want to communicate is that children can make choices about how they behave.

The story and the questions that follow the story provide an opportunity to examine factors that could cause children to lie. The anecdote also looks at the likely repercussions of lying and at how Haley's mother deals with her daughter's behavior. By helping your students understand another child's maladaptive conduct and by encouraging them to consider how this conduct can be altered, you're affirming that problems are fixable and that children can devise practical methods for handling predicaments, temptations, and value judgments. These insights provide children with a powerful resource for avoiding the type of crisis that Haley confronts in the anecdote.

As is the case in all of the units in this program, Haley's story isn't exclusively directed at children who are lying. It's also aimed at youngsters who may be affected by a classmate's conduct. Certainly, the common visceral reaction of children who are lied to by their peers is one of disillusionment and resentment. No one enjoys being victimized. By helping your students understand the feelings, thoughts, and motivations of the child who lies, you are certainly not encouraging them to condone the misbehavior. Rather, you're making students more aware of the factors that could impel a child to lie, and you're helping those children who are violating the conventions of acceptable social behavior to become more insightful about the implications and consequences of their conduct.

THE QUESTIONS THAT FOLLOW THE STORY

See page 10 for suggestions about how to present the questions that help students carefully examine the story and understand the key issues. The procedural template is essentially the same for every unit in this program.

For Students

The Child Who Tells Lies

THE STORY

1 Haley couldn't wait to talk with her best friend during
2 recess. She wanted to tell Tyisha about the wallet she had
3 found. It was filled with lots of money, and Haley wanted to
4 talk to Tyisha about what she planned to do with the money.

5 Haley had decided to save some of the money, but she
6 also wanted to buy things that her mom wouldn't let her
7 have. She wanted to buy new clothes for her favorite doll,
8 a pen that mixed colors together, and a pair of shoes with
9 wheels in the heel. She wasn't quite sure how to hide these
10 things from her mother once she actually bought them, but
11 she was certain that she could come up with a plan.

12 When Haley told Tyisha about the money, her friend's
13 eyes got very wide. "How much was in the wallet?" Tyisha
14 excitedly asked.

15 "Sixty-two dollars."

16 "Are you going to tell your mother that you found it?"

17 "No way. I'm going to keep the money and throw the
18 wallet in the garbage can."

19 "You know your mom would want you to return the wal-
20 let. If she finds out that you didn't tell her about it, she'll be
21 real angry," Tyisha warned.

22 "She won't find out. I've got a plan, but you have to
23 promise me that you won't say anything."

Haley tells Tyisha her secret.

24   "OK," Tyisha replied.

25   Haley and Tyisha spent the next five minutes talking about
26   Haley's plan for spending the money. When other children
27   wandered over to find out what the girls were discussing,
28   Haley and Tyisha changed the subject until the girls left.

29   Sixty-two dollars was a lot of money, and it was excit-
30   ing for the girls to decide how to spend it without Haley's
31   mother finding out. Neither of the girls discussed returning
32   the money to the person who had lost it.

33   "Can I see the money?" Tyisha asked eagerly.

34   "I didn't bring all of it to school, but I can show you a
35   ten-dollar bill."

36   Haley looked around to see if anyone was watching.
37   Convinced that no one was paying attention to what they
38   were doing, she reached in her pocket and pulled out the
39   ten-dollar bill.

40   Then the bell rang announcing the end of recess, and
41   the girls ran to line up. When they were back in the class-
42   room, Haley smiled at her friend who was seated in the
43   row next to hers. Tyisha smiled back. It would be so much
44   fun to buy things, Tyisha thought, and she hoped that

The wallet Haley found.

45 Haley would also let her buy something she wanted with
46 the found money. After all, she was Haley's best friend.

47 That evening, Tyisha began to feel bad. When she
48 thought about the situation, she decided that it would be
49 wrong for Haley to keep the money. She also realized that
50 her own parents would be very disappointed with her if
51 she took part and didn't try to stop Haley from keeping the
52 money. The following day as they were lining up to go to
53 class, Tyisha told her friend that she needed to talk with
54 her during recess.

55 "Where's the wallet now?" Tyisha asked after the girls
56 had moved away from the other children on the playground.

57 "I hid it in a box in the closet," Haley replied after she had
58 looked to make certain that no other children could hear.

59 "I think you should tell your mom that you found the
60 wallet. Keeping the money is like stealing," Tyisha said in
61 a low voice.

62 "No it's not! I didn't steal the wallet. The woman lost it,
63 and it's finders, keepers," Haley replied angrily.

64 "I guess," Tyisha answered. Still, she wasn't convinced.
65 "You know the person who lost the wallet will be very sad."

66 "So what! I found it, and I can keep it," Haley said
67 irritably. "And don't forget, you promised not to tell."

68 "I wish you'd never told me about the wallet," Tyisha replied.

69 With that, Haley marched off in a huff. She was clearly
70 angry with her friend whom she had expected to agree
71 with her.

72 Tyisha didn't know what to do. The excitement that she
73 had felt about helping Haley spend the money had worn
74 off. Even though she wasn't the one who had found the
75 wallet, she still felt guilty just knowing about Haley's plan.
76 She thought about it all day, and she could barely con-
77 centrate on her school work. When school was over,
78 Haley came up to Tyisha on the front lawn.

79 "Don't forget. You promised not to say anything. If you tell
80 someone, I won't be your friend," she warned. Haley then
81 turned and walked away. Tyisha saw her climb the steps
82 onto the school bus.

83 Tyisha lived only a few blocks from school. As usual,
84 Tyisha joined two of her friends who lived on the same
85 block, and they began to walk home together. Usually, the
86 girls would talk about things that happened at school, but
87 today Tyisha said very little. She was thinking about the
88 big mistake that Haley was making. Tyisha felt that she
89 had to do something, but she couldn't decide what. She
90 had promised her friend not to say anything, and promises
91 were important to Tyisha.

92 When Haley returned home from school, she went
93 directly to her room. She wanted to make sure the money
94 was still in the box where she had hidden it. She also
95 wanted to look at the money and count it again.

96 Later that afternoon, Whitney, Haley's teenage sister,
97 asked their mom if she could go to the mall to buy the pair
98 of jeans that her mother had promised her. Haley asked if
99 she could go with her sister to the mall.

100 "I don't want Haley tagging along!" Whitney said irritably.

101   "Well, I've got shopping to do at the supermarket, and
102 then I need to go to the hardware store. Whitney, you
103 either take Haley with you, or you can't go," her mother
104 said firmly. "I'll drop you girls off, and I'll pick you up in front
105 of the Emporium at 5:45. I don't want to have to wait for
106 you. I've got dinner to cook."

107   Whitney was unhappy about the idea of having to take
108 Haley with her to the mall, but she had no choice. Haley
109 smiled when her mother announced that she had to go
110 along. When her mother's back was turned, Haley made a
111 silly face at Whitney and stuck out her tongue. This made
112 Whitney even more angry.

113   When their mom dropped them off, the girls went to
114 Whitney's favorite clothing store. After trying on six pairs
115 of jeans, Whitney finally found what she wanted.

116   As the two girls walked through the mall on their way to
117 the Emporium, Haley asked her sister if she could go into
118 a toy store. Whitney looked at her watch and shrugged.

119   "I suppose it's OK. We still have about twenty minutes until
120 Mom gets here," Whitney said without much enthusiasm.

121   After entering the toy store, Haley wandered over to
122 the doll section. She picked out a new outfit for her doll,
123 and she told her sister that she was going to buy it. She
124 then pulled a twenty-dollar bill from her pocket.

125   "Where did you get this money?" Whitney asked.

126   "I saved it," Haley replied.

127   "No way," Whitney said.

128   "I did! I really did," Haley insisted.

129   "You sure you didn't take that money from Mom's
130 purse?" Whitney asked suspiciously.

131   "No, I swear. Just don't tell Mom that I bought the
132 clothes. She'll get mad."

133
134
"I don't know. If she finds out, then she'll get mad at me for not saying something."

135
"Please! Promise me you won't tell her."

136
"I'll think about it," Whitney replied.

137
138
139
140
141
142
Haley paid for the doll clothes, and the girls started to walk to where they would meet their mother. While Whitney was looking in a store window, Haley secretly took the doll clothes from the plastic bag and dropped the empty bag into a trashcan. She then put the folded doll clothes in her jacket pocket.

143
144
145
146
147
That evening, after she and her sister cleared off the dinner table and put the plates and utensils in the dishwasher, Haley went to her room to do her homework. After about twenty minutes, her mother knocked on the door and came in.

148
149
150
151
152
"I want to talk to you, Haley. Whitney told me that you had a twenty-dollar bill and that you bought some doll clothes at the mall this afternoon," her mother said. She had a stern look on her face. "Where did you get the twenty dollars, Haley?"

153
154
Haley gulped. Her sister had told! For a moment she didn't know what to say.

155
156
157
"Tyisha found a wallet with money inside, and she gave me some," Haley finally replied. She was staring down at her desk.

158
159
"Oh, really?" her mom said. "And where did she find the wallet?"

160
161
"She found it in the street," Haley replied in a low voice. She began to tremble slightly.

162
163
"Does her mother know that she found this wallet?"

164
"Yes. She told Tyisha that she could keep the money."

165 "Hmm," Haley's mother said in a disbelieving tone. "I
166 think I need to check this story out."

167 Haley's mom went back to the kitchen. Haley could
168 hear her pick up the phone and begin to dial. Haley felt
169 desperate. She wanted to run away, but there was no
170 place to run. She tried to listen to what her mother was
171 saying, but because her room was down the hall, she
172 could only hear some of the words. Haley thought about
173 going into the kitchen, but she decided not to. She didn't
174 want to be there when her mother heard the truth.

175 A few minutes later, Haley's mother came into Haley's
176 room. She had a very stern look on her face.

177 "Haley, Tyisha says you were the one who found the
178 wallet. She apparently told her mother about it when she
179 came home from school."

180 "I didn't find it," Haley mumbled. She couldn't look at
181 her mother. "Tyisha gave me the money to buy the doll
182 clothes. She has the wallet."

183 "Are you telling me the truth?"

184 "Yes!"

185 "Come with me, Haley," her mom said in a firm voice.

186 Haley's mom led Haley down the hall and into the
187 garage. She picked up an old newspaper and spread it on
188 the floor. Then she did something that Haley would never
189 have expected her to do. She dumped the garbage on the
190 newspaper. Tyisha must have told her mom that Haley had
191 thrown the wallet in the trash! The wallet was in plain view.
192 Haley's mom put on a rubber glove and picked it up. She
193 then took a damp sponge and cleaned it off.

194 "You lied to me, Haley. You were the one who found the
195 wallet, and you were the one who decided to keep the
196 money. And then you lied and blamed everything on
197 Tyisha."

198 "I'm sorry," Haley sobbed. Tears were rolling down her
199 cheeks.

Haley's mother asks her if she is telling the truth.

200   "Haley, this is not the first time that I've caught you
201 lying. This is very serious. You not only lied to me, but you
202 were planning to keep this woman's money. That's steal-
203 ing. Then you threw this woman's wallet in the garbage.
204 Her driver's license, her credit cards, and photos of her
205 children and her husband are in the wallet, as well as
206 other papers that must be very important to her. All of this
207 would have ended up in the garbage dump. And equally
208 upsetting is the fact that you were willing to blame your
209 best friend for something that you did."

210   "I'm sorry," Haley repeated. It was all she could think of
211 saying.

212   "Well, that's a start, but it's not good enough to simply
213 say you're sorry. What you did was very wrong. I believe
214 you're sorry mainly because you got caught, but I'm not
215 convinced that you wouldn't do the same thing again if
216 you had the chance."

217   "I promise I won't, Mommy!"

218   "I'm going to make sure of it. How much money was in
219 the wallet?"

220   "Sixty-two dollars."

221   "Go get me the remaining money right now."

222 Haley went to get the money. She was still sobbing. As
223 she passed Whitney's room, she could see her sister look-
224 ing at her. Whitney shook her head back and forth as her
225 sister walked past her door. Haley went to her hiding place
226 and scooped up the rest of the money.

227 "You have forty-two dollars here. How much did the doll
228 clothes cost?" her mother asked when Haley returned to
229 the kitchen.

230 "Twelve dollars and fifty-two cents," Haley replied in a
231 low voice.

232 "Where is the change?" Haley's mother asked sternly.

233 "In my coat pocket."

234 "Go get it now."

235 Haley went back to her room to get the money. Tears
236 were still running down her face.

237 "Haley, I am going to replace the money you spent on
238 the doll clothes, and I'm going to put the sixty-two dollars
239 back in the wallet. You will repay me the money you spent
240 by doing chores during the next two months. Now you're
241 going to speak to the woman who lost the wallet. I will get
242 her phone number from the telephone book. You will tell
243 her that you found her wallet and the money and that your
244 mother will be driving you to her house to return it. After
245 you speak to the woman, you will then call Tyisha. You'll
246 tell her mother that you were the one who found the wal-
247 let and kept the money, and you will apologize for lying.
248 You will tell her that Tyisha had nothing to do with it. Then
249 you will ask to speak with Tyisha, and you will apologize to
250 her for lying, for trying to get her in trouble, and for not
251 being a good friend."

252 "Mommy, please, couldn't you make the calls for me?"

253 "Absolutely not. You made this mess, and you will have
254 to take responsibility for cleaning it up. You also need to

255 know that you're grounded for the next four weekends.
256 That means no playdates, no TV, no riding your bicycle,
257 no skating, and no going to the movies. This lying must
258 stop now. Do you understand me, young lady?"

259 "Yes," Haley replied in a voice that could barely be
260 heard.

261 "OK. Repeat what the consequences are that I have
262 just described."

263 Haley repeated the list of consequences, and her
264 mother wrote them down on a piece of paper. Then her
265 mother picked up the telephone book and found the
266 number of the woman who had lost the wallet. After Haley
267 was done speaking with the woman, Haley's mother
268 reminded her daughter that she still had one more tele-
269 phone call to make. Haley dreaded making this call. She
270 felt so embarrassed. She was sorry that she had ever
271 found the wallet. How horribly everything had turned out.
272 One thing was certain—the eight-year-old knew that she
273 was done lying. She had learned a very, very painful les-
274 son, and now she needed to prove to her mother that she
275 could be trusted again.

ORAL QUESTIONS

■ Why do you think Haley told Tyisha about finding the wallet?

Function: *Developing analytical and critical thinking skills.*

Comments: The types of responses you're looking for include:*

- She needed to tell someone about what she had done.
- She wanted to impress Tyisha with all of the money she had found.
- She wanted to show Tyisha that she could get away with keeping the money.
- She wanted to show her friend that she didn't care about what her mother would do.
- She wanted to hear Tyisha's ideas about what to buy with the money.
- She wanted to make her friend jealous.

*As previously noted in other units, you don't need to elicit all of these reasons. Be prepared for off-target or illogical responses. These should be treated with sensitivity. As students participate in these class discussions, their reasoning and analytical thinking skills will improve. You want to create a safe context in which students feel that they can freely express their ideas and feelings.

■ What words would you use to describe Haley? Explain why you've chosen these words.

Function: *Developing observational skills, perceptiveness, and analytical thinking skills.*

Comments: The types of responses you're looking for include:

- Lies
- Dishonest
- Not smart
- Willing to take risks
- Unafraid of consequences
- A show-off

■ Why do you think Haley believed that it was OK to keep the money?

Function: *Developing analytical thinking skills.*

Comments: The types of responses you're looking for include:

- She didn't know the person who had lost it.
- If you find something, you can keep it (finders, keepers).
- She thought no one would find out that she found the wallet and kept the money.

> - She didn't know the difference between right and wrong.
> - She wanted to buy things with the money so badly that she convinced herself that what she was doing was all right.
> - She didn't care about other people's feelings.

■ Why do you think Tyisha told Haley that she should give the money back?

> **Function: *Developing analytical thinking skills and empathy.***
>
> **Comments:** The types of responses you are looking for include:
>
> - She realized that keeping the money was wrong.
> - She felt sorry for the person who had lost the wallet.
> - She wanted to prevent her friend from making a mistake.
> - She thought her friend was going to get into trouble.
> - She thought that she herself might get into trouble because she knew what had happened.

■ Is there anything that Tyisha could have done to handle the problem?

> **Function: *Developing analytical and critical thinking skills and insight and learning to brainstorm and problem solve. (You may want to use the brainstorming tree on page 12.)***
>
> **Comments:** The types of responses you are looking for include:
>
> - She could tell her mother about what happened.
> - She could tell Haley's mother about what happened.
> - She could tell the teacher about what happened.
> - She could tell Haley that she would have to tell her mom if Haley didn't give back the money and the wallet.
> - She could call Haley and try again to convince her to return the money.

■ Why do you think Tyisha began to feel bad that evening, and why did she wish that Haley had never told her about the money?

> **Function: *Developing analytical and critical thinking skills, insight, and empathy.***
>
> **Comments:** The types of responses you're looking for include:
>
> - She realized that keeping the money was wrong.
> - She felt Haley was making a mistake.

- By telling her what she had done, Haley involved Tyisha in the scheme.
- She felt guilty for having thought about the things she could buy if Haley gave her some of the money.
- She wanted to do something to stop Haley from keeping the money, but she didn't know what to do.
- She felt sorry that she had promised Haley that she wouldn't say anything.
- She was struggling with whether to break the promise and tell an adult about the wallet and the money.

■ If your friend convinces you to promise to keep a secret that you know would be wrong to keep, can you do something about it?

Function: *Enhancing analytical and critical thinking skills.*

Comments: The types of responses you're looking for include:

- You can tell your friend that you can't keep the promise because it would be wrong to do so.
- You could explain to your friend that you could get into trouble if you keep the promise.
- You could explain to your friend why he's making a serious mistake.
- You could warn your friend that you'll have to tell an adult about the situation.
- You could try to persuade your friend to do what's right.
- You could tell your friend that it's not fair to tell you about something that's wrong and then expect you to keep a promise not to tell anyone.

■ In what situations would you be justified in breaking a promise to a friend?

Function: *Enhancing analytical and critical thinking skills.*

Comments: The types of responses you're looking for include:

- Your friend tells you that he's throwing rocks at cars.
- Your friend tells you that she's going to steal something from a store.
- Your friend tells you he's going to cheat on a test.
- Your friend tells you that she's smoking cigarettes.
- Your friend tells you that a family member is abusing him.
- Your friend tells you that her older brother is selling drugs to children at school.
- Your friend tells you about a child who is being bullied by an older child.

■ Why do you think children lie?

> **Function: *Enhancing analytical and critical thinking skills.***
>
> **Comments:** The types of responses you're looking for include:
>
> - Their parents may not have taught them that lying is wrong.
> - They want to avoid getting into trouble.
> - They lie so that they can get what they want.
> - They want to impress other children.
> - They believe that they can get away with lying.
> - They don't care about hurting other people with their lies.
> - They don't care about the consequences if they're caught lying.

■ Can you think of situations that might cause a child to be tempted to lie?

> **Function: *Developing analytical thinking skills.***
>
> **Comments:** The types of responses you're looking for include:
>
> - You find a watch in the park that you want to keep. You think about lying to your parents and telling them that your friend gave it to you.
> - You take something from another child's desk. Your teacher tells your parents about what you did. You think about lying and telling your parents that you didn't do it.
> - You forget to hand in your homework, and your teacher calls your parents. You think about lying to them and telling them you really did hand in the assignment.
> - You break a neighbor's window, and the neighbor calls your parents. You think about lying to your parents and telling them another child broke the window.

■ What could a child do to resist the temptation to lie?

> **Function: *Developing analytical thinking skills, strategic thinking skills, and heightened awareness and insight.***
>
> **Comments:** The types of responses you're looking for include:
>
> - He could remind himself that lying is wrong.
> - She could remind herself that she should act in ways that make her proud of herself.
> - He could think about the consequences and punishments for lying.
> - She could remind herself that her parents would be very disappointed and upset if she lied to them.

■ Why would parents be concerned if their child tells lies?

> **Function: *Developing analytical, evaluative, and expressive language skills and empathy.***
>
> **Comments:** The types of responses you're looking for include:
>
> - They would be concerned that the lies would get their child into trouble.
> - They would be concerned that their child would lose her friends.
> - They would be concerned that no one would ever believe what their child says.
> - They would be embarrassed by their child's behavior.
> - They would be concerned that others would consider them to be bad parents.
> - They would be concerned that their child might lie whenever it's easier for him to do so.

■ What are some of the consequences of lying?

> **Function: *Developing analytical, evaluative, and critical thinking skills.***
>
> **Comments:** The types of responses you're looking for include:
>
> - Never being believed
> - Losing your friends
> - Making your parents angry
> - Disappointing your parents
> - Making your teachers angry
> - Disappointing your teachers
> - Getting into trouble
> - Being punished
> - Not being trusted

OPTIONAL ACTIVITY: CAREFUL READING AND ANALYSIS OF THE STORY

(These exercises are designed for students who can read at the second-grade level and above.)

- In the story, Tyisha was tempted at first to ask Haley to give her some of the money from the wallet. Go back and find the sentence that describes the temptation and underline it one time. (Hint: You can find the sentence in lines 44 to 46.)

- Even though Tyisha had not taken the money, she felt bad. Underline the sentence that describes how she was feeling. Then underline two times the two sentences that tell why Tyisha began to feel bad that evening. (Hint: You can find the sentences in lines 47 to 52.)

- The following day, Tyisha told Haley that she should return the money and explained why she felt that way. Haley refused, and she gave her own reason for keeping the money. Underline the sentence in which Tyisha explained why the money should be returned one time and underline Haley's reason for keeping the money two times. (Hint: You can find these sentences in lines 59 to 63.)

- Haley threatened to do something if Tyisha told anyone about the money. Find and underline the sentence in the story that describes what she threatened to do. (Hint: You can find the sentence in lines 79 to 80.)

- When Whitney asked Haley about the twenty-dollar bill that she used to pay for the doll clothes, Haley told her sister a lie. Find and underline the lie that she told Whitney. (Hint: You can find the sentence in lines 125 to 127.)

- After Whitney told their mother about the money that her sister used to pay for the doll clothes, Haley's mom came into Haley's room to ask where she got the money. Haley told her mother a lie. Go back into the story and find the lie that Haley told her mother. (Hint: You can find the sentence in lines 153 to 157.)

- Haley's mother called Tyisha's mother to see if Haley's story was true. The story didn't check out, and Haley's mother told her daughter what Tyisha had said about the wallet. Haley then told her mother another lie. Go back into the story and underline the second lie Haley told her mother. (Hint: You can find the sentences in lines 177 to 182.)

- To get to the truth, Haley's mom did something in the garage. Find the sentences that describe what Haley's mother did. (Hint: You can find the sentences in lines 185 to 193.)

- Haley's mom replaced the sixty-two dollars, and she insisted that her daughter do certain things. Underline each of the steps that her mother insisted that she take. (Hint: Look in lines 237 to 252, and see if you can find eight steps. All of the steps are in one paragraph.)

- Haley's mom grounded Haley for four weeks. Underline the other five punishments. (Hint: You can find the sentences describing the punishments in lines 252 to 258.)

- After this run-in with her mother, there was a major change in Haley's attitude about lying. Because she had lied several times in the past, Haley realized that she would have to prove her truthfulness to her mom. Underline the sentence that describes what she decided. (Hint: You can find the sentence describing her decision in lines 271 to 275.)

SUPPLEMENTAL REPRODUCIBLE EXERCISES

(These reinforcement exercises can be completed in class or assigned for homework.)

❑ **If you were tempted to lie about something, what could you do to stop yourself from doing so? Write your ideas in the space below.**

1. _____

2. _____

3. _____

4. _____

❑ **Rate the decision by Haley's mother to have her daughter personally return the wallet and the money to the woman who lost the wallet.**

Using a Scale

If you've forgotten how to use a scale to rate something, look back on page 25.

Choose the number that best describes what you think about the idea of Haley having to speak to the woman who lost the wallet and then go to her house to return it.

1	2	3	4	5	6	7	8	9	10
Poor				Average					Excellent

❑ **Why did you choose the number that you circled?**

_____

_____

_____

_____

❑ **Do you think that Haley will continue to lie?   Yes   No**

If you answered "yes," explain your reasons in the space below.

_____

_____

_____

If you answered "no," explain your reasons in the space below.

_____

_____

_____

❑ **If you knew that a child in your class was lying to get someone in trouble, what could you do about it?**

1. _____

2. _____

3. _____

❑ **Would you feel guilty about reporting a student who was telling a serious lie? Yes   No**

If you answered "yes," explain your reasons for feeling guilty in the space below.

_____

_____

_____

If you answered "no," explain your reasons for not feeling guilty in the space below.

_____

_____

_____

❑ **Would you be willing to break a promise if you later decided that keeping the promise was wrong?   Yes   No**

If you answered "yes," explain your reasons in the space below.

_____

_____

_____

If you answered "no," explain your reasons in the space below.

_____

_____

_____

❑ **List some reasons a punishment for telling lies might be good for the child who is being punished.**

1. _____

2. _____

3. _____

Would you be willing to be friends with a child who often lies to you? Yes   No

If you answered "yes," explain your reasons in the space below.

_____

_____

_____

If you answered "no," explain your reasons in the space below.

_____

_____

_____

FOLLOW-UP AND APPLICATION

Despite having extensively examined the issue of truthfulness with your students, you may not see immediate behavioral changes in children who are in the habit of lying. As repeatedly noted in this program, negative conduct patterns can be difficult to break, and some youngsters may persist in being untruthful.

Follow-up and reinforcement are critical components in the process of achieving meaningful behavioral change. In a nonpreachy way, you should remind students about the importance of being truthful. Those who lie should be privately alerted when you become aware of their untruthfulness. Be prepared for denials and justifications. For this reason, it's important to have personally verified that the lying did, in fact, occur or to have corroboration if a child reports that another child is lying.

Students must be periodically reminded that there are not-to-be-broken conduct rules and that there are serious consequences for breaking these rules. These consequences might include calling the child's parents, having a conference with the child's parents, or, if there continue to be repeated incidences of lying, referring the child to the school counselor or a school district psychologist or social worker. If the lying is chronic, it could reflect underlying psychological issues that may require intervention by a mental health professional.

At the same time, you must privately acknowledge and affirm students who are making positive behavioral changes and becoming more truthful. Let them know that you are aware that they are no longing telling lies and that you are pleased and proud of them.

CONCRETE REINFORCEMENTS

You might have children break up into small groups and have each group create some simple posters. One might state, "You should not lie." Another might list the consequences of lying: Lying will cause you to lose friends, upset the teacher, disappoint your parents, and get you into trouble. These posters will serve as tangible reminders of the issues that were examined in the unit. You could affix the posters to a "messages to students" wall and periodically have the entire class read one or more of the posters aloud in unison. This reinforcement is a critically important component of the cognitive behavioral change model. When your students are tempted to lie, you want them to have an imprinted automatic negative association with being untruthful.

Your objective is for your students to understand the reasons why certain conduct is wrong and cannot be condoned. You also want them to be aware of the impact their behavior can have on others. Providing acknowledgment and praise for children who stop lying is an essential element in the behavioral change process. Your acknowledgment and praise for resisting the temptation to be untruthful should obviously be provided privately, because you certainly wouldn't want to publicly embarrass the child who lies.

As a further reinforcement, you could have students do skits that recap the issues that they've examined and discussed. For example, in the skit a child (definitely not a student who has actually been lying) would tell a lie. For example, the child might say that a famous baseball player came to dinner the previous night. The other students might at first believe the child. Then another student might say it would be impossible for Alex Rodriguez or Derek Jeter to come to dinner that night, because both teams were on road trips. The children might then shun the child who told the lie, and when he tries to play with them, they might shake their heads and ignore him.

Enhancing students' awareness of important rules of conduct and of the consequences for breaking these rules is a vital step in preparing them to deal successfully with society's covenants. Children must understand that society does not tolerate liars.

Teaching children not to lie is an unequivocally attainable goal if the reorientation process begins early enough and the behavioral change procedures are fundamentally sound and consistently applied. Strengthening students' awareness of socially acceptable values, explicit strictures, and cause-and-effect principles is also an unequivocally attainable goal, and enhancing students' analytical, strategic thinking, and problem-solving skills is unquestionably doable. With effective instruction, guidance, and mentoring, these objectives can be achieved, and the impact of your efforts on your students' lives will be profound and lasting.

Unit 5

The Child Who Is a Bully

For Educators

*Examining the Dynamics
and Implications of Bullying*

Children who bully other children do so because they're angry, insecure, socially inept, or unpopular. By intimidating and terrorizing children who are weaker and more vulnerable, they are able to vent their frustration and compensate for their feelings of inadequacy. Control and power function as a surrogate for social sufficiency.

Despite the transparency of the bully's antisocial conduct, children resorting to this cruel and aggressive behavior rarely are consciously aware of the underlying factors that impel them to menace other children. Most do not realize that they're angry and feel inferior. The bully's mind simply latches onto an available means for handling his social dysfunctionality and angst, a means predicated on asserting power and control. Children who bully, whether they are boys or girls, are oblivious to an obvious irony: Their conduct draws attention to the very deficiencies they are trying to camouflage, underscores their maladjustment, and precludes any possibility of social acceptance.

The pain that bullies inflict on their victims is invariably profound, and the targets of their harassment may become so fearful and distraught that they dread going to school. To avoid having to confront the bully, some victims will complain of stomachaches and sore throats and implore their parent to allow them to stay home from school. When they are at school, they may make up excuses for their being allowed to remain in the classroom during recess, or they may hover near the playground or lunchroom supervisor. The victimized child's palpable fear can so dominate his life that he thinks of nothing else, and all the while the child's parents and teacher may be unaware of what's happening. The child may be too terrorized and intimidated to say anything. This reticence is especially prevalent when the bully has threatened to harm him further if he tells anyone about what's happening.

POWER AS A SURROGATE SOCIAL ACCEPTANCE

In some respects, the bully's self-defeating behavior parallels that of a socially inept adult with poor self-esteem who goes to a party, drinks too much, acts obnoxiously, and discovers that the other guests are convinced that he's a fool and take pains to avoid interacting with him. Unconsciously driven by his insecurities to sabotage himself, the man's maladaptive behavior and the ensuing social rejection reinforce his feelings of inferiority and further diminish his already tenuous self-concept. In effect, the party drunk shoots himself in the foot.

Most bullies don't recognize that they, too, are shooting themselves in the foot. Many are too psychologically defended to acknowledge their feelings of inadequacy and hostility and to realize that their conduct estranges them from their peers and precludes social acceptance. These children are blind to an immutable cause-and-effect dynamic: People who threaten, intimidate, and terrorize are loathed and ostracized. Even children who are not personally victimized usually feel nothing but contempt for bullies. They may not proactively take a stand against the bully, but most are repulsed by the conduct.

In many instances, the bully's malevolent behavior can be successfully reoriented through timely and skillful teacher intervention. This intervention comprises asserting clearly defined rules of conduct, imposing consistent and unequivocal consequences for misconduct, and applying an effective instructional methodology to help children achieve greater insight into their behavior. The goal is to help the bully realize that his peers and teachers recognize his antisocial behavior, that this behavior is self-defeating and hurtful, and that it won't be countenanced. The bottom line is that bullies must be stopped before they damage other children.

The most obvious means for stopping bullies is to draw a clear line in the sand and to say, "No more! Bullying at this school will not be tolerated." Supplementing the "no bullying permitted" dictum with instruction to help the bully realize that by altering his behavior, he can achieve the social acceptance that he craves plays an equally pivotal role in the conduct-reorientation process. The goal of this cognitive behavioral change strategy is to lead the bully to the realization that the payoffs for acting civilized are far more gratifying than any payoffs that might be derived from intimidating, controlling, extorting, and harassing other children.

Bullying becomes even more insidious when socially disenfranchised children band together to form a gang with the primary objective of intimidating and exploiting defenseless children. The gang provides its socially alienated members with an identity, and the shared gang mentality supports the malevolent behavior of the gang's members. In effect, the gang dynamic affirms that it's OK to be cruel. Assaulting students on the way to school or on the way home from school, demanding money, menacing children on the playground, and reveling in the feelings of dominance that brute force induces can become standard operating procedure.

Causing fear and imposing control provide the unconscious psychological "glue" that holds the bully's world together. The bully's behavior asserts the following beliefs:

- I'm strong.
- I'm dominant.
- I'm in control.

- I can intimidate you with impunity.
- I can make your life miserable if you don't acquiesce to my demands.
- No one can protect you.

This mind-set was clearly operative in the personalities of the social outcasts who precipitated the tragedy at Columbine High School. Certainly, other factors also played key roles in causing the carnage at Columbine, namely, social rejection, feelings of alienation, overpowering anger, frustration, and increasing emotional dysfunction. A renegade "we against them" mentality evolved. Plaintive cries for help disguised as bravado were either not heard or simply disregarded by parents, school authorities, and police, the very people who might have interceded and prevented the subsequent tragedy. Menacing, nihilistic behavior camouflaged the pain of the two perpetrators. On the surface, the teenagers proclaimed through their behavior and their dress, "Hey, we're dangerous outlaws, and you had better fear us. We will punish those who have rejected and belittled us. We are lethal and indomitable. Watch out." Beneath this delusional proclamation was a more sobering and sorrowful message: "No one understands us or cares about us. We're teetering out of control, and no one seems capable of stopping us." Perhaps these narcissistic traits were already evident when these teenagers were in elementary school, and perhaps certain aware teachers and administrators recognized and flagged the potential danger, but it's clear that the effective intervention that might have averted the carnage was never provided.

The historical antecedents of the bully phenomenon in its extreme are well documented. The world's most malevolent tyrants were at the core bullies who were driven by the compelling need to control and terrorize. One might speculate whether the incipient twisted and virulent personality traits of psychopathic despots such as Hitler, Stalin, Mussolini, Pol Pot, Idi Amin, and Saddam Hussein and their complete absence of conscience, empathy, and compassion might have been discernable to their first- and second-grade teachers.

No one is suggesting that the eight-year-old bully in your class is a budding sociopath or psychopath, but clearly red flags are flapping, and these danger signals must be heeded. The conduct of children who tyrannize other children poses a distinct risk to those who are being tyrannized, and decisive intervention is essential. In many cases, an insightful teacher equipped with an effective cognitive behavioral change strategy (see pages xii–xiii) may be able to successfully reorient the emerging antisocial behavior. In extreme and intransigent cases, an assessment by a mental health professional is vital.

TRAINING CHILDREN TO BE KIND

Children possess the potential to be kind and the potential to be cruel. Their conduct is a reflection of their personalities, upbringing, life experiences, and psychological and neurological hardwiring. If left unchecked, a propensity for cruelty can become standard operating procedure. Unless this conduct is vigorously, consistently, and effectively discouraged, the malevolence could become an ingrained habit.

The primary responsibility for guiding children to a greater awareness of their own behavior and its impact on others rightfully rests on parents' shoulders, but teachers also share some of this responsibility. The obligation to provide guidance is especially compelling when teachers conclude that a child's parents aren't doing their job effectively.

Enhancing your students' awareness of the boundaries (e.g., "This behavior is acceptable, and this behavior is not acceptable, and these are the reasons why") can play a key role in teaching children to recognize and conform to society's basic values and strictures. The alternative is to allow behaviors such as bullying to persist unchecked. The short- and long-range consequences of this failure to intercede are likely to prove disastrous—not only for the bully, but also for society. Unless there is effective and opportune intervention, childhood bullies are likely to become adult bullies.

THE ROLE OF THE TEACHER

Establishing externally imposed and consistently enforced limits and clearly defining explicit consequences for misconduct are core elements in helping children internalize the boundaries and acquire essential social inhibitions. Students must realize that they're obligated to conform to rules in the classroom, on the playground, and in the lunchroom, and one of the core injunctions is not to be cruel to other children. Those who transgress must be cautioned and reprimanded or punished. They also should ideally be provided with an opportunity to gain greater insight into their deleterious behavior and its impact on others. These are core elements in the cognitive behavioral change methods that are a thematic constant in this program.

Given the risks to the emotional and physical well-being of the bully's victims, teachers have a compelling responsibility to be vigilant. As noted in the preceding unit that addresses the issue of lies, elementary school teachers cannot escape the responsibility to act in loco parentis (i.e., as parental stand-ins) when the situation requires that they do so. They must proactively, decisively, and skillfully intercede if they observe or even suspect that children are being cruel to other children. No child should have to experience the terror and indignity of being victimized.

EXAMINING THE STORY

The student-directed story and the analytical thinking activities in this unit are designed to expand your students' level of consciousness vis-à-vis bullying. The description of the protagonist's behavior should resonate not only in the child who is being tyrannized but also in the child who is doing the tyrannizing. (*Please note:* To make the following examination of the issues more concrete, you may want to skip ahead and read the story.)

The anecdote describes the pain a child who is being terrorized by a bully experiences every day. The story clearly affirms that most problems can be fixed, even problems that appear to a child to be overwhelming and insoluble.

Children who are being abused must be guided to the realization that their parents and teacher are their first line of defense against bullying and that they should feel safe confiding in them when they're being threatened or exploited. This message is not only relevant to reporting a bully, but is equally relevant to reporting anyone, be it another child or an adult, who is acting suspiciously, menacingly, or exploitively.

The story and questions in this unit provide your students with an opportunity to examine the causal factors and implications of bullying. The anecdote examines the protagonist's feelings of powerlessness and describes how his parents and the school administration deal with the crisis. Your students learn that they have potent adult allies who will not permit them to be victimized. By guiding children to key insights about bullying and by encouraging them to consider how they can respond in ways that neutralize the bully's power, you're empowering your students and furnishing them with tangible and accessible options for protecting themselves.

THE QUESTIONS THAT FOLLOW THE STORY

See Unit 1 (page 10) for suggestions about how to present the questions that help students carefully examine the story and understand the key issues. The recommended procedural template is essentially the same for all of the units in this program.

For Students

The Child Who Is a Bully

THE STORY

1   Caleb looked at the clock and watched the second
2 hand moving. Recess would be in ten minutes, and Caleb
3 desperately wished that he could stop the hands of the
4 clock from going forward. Unlike his classmates, Caleb
5 dreaded recess because he knew what would happen on
6 the playground.

7   When the clock finally said 10:45, Ms. Reston told the
8 students to line up for recess. The children then marched
9 out the door and down the hall to the playground. They
10 were finally free for fifteen minutes of fun.

11   As soon as Ms. Reston's back was turned, Lucas
12 grabbed Caleb's arm and led him to an area that the
13 teacher couldn't see from where she was standing.

14   "Do you have a present for me today?" Lucas snarled.

15   Then Lucas reached into Caleb's pocket and took his
16 milk money. The same thing happened every day.

17   Sometimes Caleb tried to hide the money. If Lucas
18 couldn't find the quarters right away, he would twist
19 Caleb's arm until Caleb could barely keep from crying.

20   "Tell me where it is, or I'll really hurt you," Lucas would
21 threaten.

22   This threat would so frighten Caleb that he would
23 immediately reach into his hiding place and give Lucas

Lucas demands Caleb's money.

24 the money. After several painful arm twists and black-and-
25 blue marks, the eight-year-old decided that it was better to
26 put the quarters in a pocket where Lucas could easily find
27 them. At least this way, his arm wouldn't be hurt.

28 Lucas always had to be on the lookout for Ms. Reston.
29 Before he approached Caleb, he would make sure she
30 was at the other end of the playground. If she wandered
31 closer or looked in his direction, Lucas would immediately
32 put his arm around Caleb's shoulder and pretend that they
33 were two friends talking.

34 Caleb was one of the smallest boys in his class, and
35 Lucas was one of the biggest. Because everyone knew that
36 Lucas was a bully, all the children avoided him. Lucas only
37 bullied the littlest kids, and Caleb was not his only victim. He
38 had also started terrorizing Ryan and Max. These boys,
39 who were also small, were in one of the other second-grade
40 classes that shared the playground during recess.

41 None of the children who were being bullied told their
42 teachers about what was happening. They were too fright-
43 ened. Lucas had said he would break their arms if they
44 said anything. Because they were so scared, they also
45 never told their parents about what Lucas was doing.

46 One day Ms. Reston asked Caleb why he never bought
47 milk in the cafeteria.

48 "I'm not allowed to drink milk. I'm allergic to it," Caleb
49 replied. This is what Lucas had told him to say if the
50 teacher ever asked about why he didn't buy milk.

51 Kyle was Caleb's best friend at school. He was much
52 bigger than Caleb, so Lucas never picked on him.

53 "Why don't you tell Ms. Reston about Lucas?" Kyle
54 asked for the hundredth time.

55 "I don't want to," Caleb replied.

56 "If you don't want to tell the teacher, then why don't you
57 tell your parents?" Kyle asked.

58 "I don't want to," Caleb repeated. Kyle knew that Caleb
59 would say this, and he knew why. Caleb was too scared to
60 say anything about what was happening. It made Kyle very
61 sad that Lucas was getting away with bullying his friend.

62 That morning during recess, Kyle watched from the
63 basketball court as Lucas went over to Caleb to take his
64 milk money. He quickly ran over to where the two boys
65 were standing.

66 "Leave him alone!" Kyle said to Lucas. His fists were
67 closed, and Lucas could see that Kyle was ready to hit him.

68 Lucas stared at Kyle and then turned to look at Caleb.
69 His face was very angry.

70 "I'll deal with you later," he hissed. He turned and
71 walked away. He had a very nasty look on his face.

72 "Why did you get him angry at me?" Caleb demanded.
73 "Now, it will be worse!"

74 "You can't let him do this all the time," Kyle said.

75 "There's nothing I can do," Caleb sobbed. Tears were
76 rolling down his cheeks. "Promise me you won't say any-
77 thing to Ms. Reston or your mom. Your mother will tell my
78 mom, and when Lucas finds out, he'll really hurt me."

79   "I won't say anything," Kyle reluctantly agreed. "But I
80 think you're making a mistake."

81   That evening Kyle was tempted to break his promise. It
82 made him very sad to see how terrified Caleb was of
83 Lucas and how mean Lucas was to his best friend. He
84 was tempted to go and sock Lucas in the nose, but then
85 he would get in trouble.

86   Parent-teacher conferences began two days later.
87 Caleb's parents arrived at 2:30 for their appointment with
88 Ms. Reston. They discussed Caleb's schoolwork and his
89 progress in school. Ms. Reston told them that Caleb's
90 reading had improved because of the extra time he and
91 his parents spent reading every evening. She also
92 reported that Caleb was one of the best spellers in the
93 class and that he was also one of the top math students.

94   "Oh, by the way, Caleb has been very good about not
95 drinking any milk," Ms. Reston said.

96   "What do you mean?" Caleb's mother asked.

Ms. Reston greeting Caleb's parents at the conference.

97 "I'm talking about Caleb's milk allergy," Ms. Reston said.

98 "What milk allergy?" Caleb's father replied in a sur-
99 prised tone.

100 "I asked Caleb why he never buys milk for lunch, and
101 he told me he's allergic to milk."

102 "No, he's not," Caleb's mom replied.

103 "Well, that's what he told me."

104 "I give him milk money every day," Caleb's mom told
105 Ms. Reston. "This is very upsetting. I wonder what he is
106 doing with the money I give him?"

107 "We need to talk to Caleb when we get home," his
108 father said sternly. "Maybe he's keeping the milk money
109 and using it for something else."

110 When Caleb's parents returned home after the confer-
111 ence, his father asked Caleb's older brother to go upstairs
112 and finish his homework.

113 "Caleb, your mom and I would like to talk with you," his
114 father said in a serious voice. "Please come into the living
115 room."

116 Caleb's father pointed to the chair where he wanted his
117 son to sit. Then he and Caleb's mom sat down.

118 "What's wrong?" Caleb asked. He could tell that his
119 parents were upset. "Did Ms. Reston say I was doing bad
120 in school?"

121 "No. In fact, she told us that you were making fine
122 progress," his mother answered. "Ms. Reston also told us
123 something else that we find very disturbing. She says that
124 you haven't been buying milk when you go to the cafeteria.
125 She told us that you said that you have a milk allergy. Your
126 dad and I want to know what's going on. Why aren't you
127 buying milk, and what are you doing with your milk money?"

128 Caleb's cheeks turned red, and tears began to roll
129 down his face. He didn't know what to say. He just looked
130 down at the floor, and he began to sob.

131
132
"Caleb, tell us what's happening," his father said in a gentle voice.

133
134
"Lucas takes my money every day!" Caleb finally blurted out.

135
"What do you mean?" his mother asked.

136
137
138
139
"He twists my arm until I give him the money. He also takes money from Ryan and Max. He's much bigger than we are, and he tells us he will break our arms if we don't give him the money or if we tell anyone."

140
141
"How long has this been going on, son?" Caleb's father asked.

142
143
"Since the beginning of school," Caleb responded in a low voice.

144
145
"Why didn't you tell us about what Lucas was doing?" Caleb's mother asked.

146
147
"Lucas said he would hurt me if I told," Caleb replied tearfully.

148
149
150
Caleb's father gently put his arms around his son and pulled him onto his lap. Caleb was still sobbing. He then tenderly stroked Caleb's head.

151
152
153
"You don't need to worry anymore, son. The bullying will stop tomorrow. We're going to deal with the problem. We'll talk to the principal in the morning. Everything will be OK."

154
155
"Lucas will be very mad. He'll twist my arm if he finds out that I told you," Caleb said in a frightened voice.

156
157
"Lucas will never bully you again. We promise," Caleb's mom said.

158
159
160
Caleb had trouble sleeping that night. He was very worried about what Lucas would do to him when he learned that Caleb had told his parents about the milk money.

161
162
The next morning, Caleb went to school with his parents. They went directly to the principal's office, and his

163 father told the secretary that they needed to speak with
164 Mrs. Rodriguez. Caleb was very nervous. He had never
165 been in the principal's office. Mrs. Rodriguez asked them
166 to sit down, and Caleb's parents told the principal about
167 Lucas. Mrs. Rodriguez seemed very upset, and she asked
168 Caleb some questions. She wrote down the names of the
169 other two boys who Lucas was bullying. Then she picked
170 up her phone and asked the vice principal to come to her
171 office. She asked him to take Caleb back to class and to
172 fill in for Ms. Reston. She wanted Ms. Reston to come to
173 her office right away and to bring Lucas with her.

174 Lucas's eyes opened wide when he saw the vice prin-
175 cipal enter the classroom with Caleb. When Lucas was
176 told that he had to go with Ms. Reston to Mrs. Rodriguez's
177 office, Caleb could see that Lucas was frightened. He
178 looked over angrily at Caleb.

179 Lucas did not return to class with Ms. Reston. When
180 Ms. Reston walked into the classroom, she headed
181 straight to Caleb's desk. She gently put her hand in
182 Caleb's shoulder and said in a low voice, "I'm very sorry

Lucas waiting outside the principal's office.

183 about what happened, Caleb. It will never happen again."
184 The other children looked at each other and started whis-
185 pering. They realized that Lucas had finally been caught.
186 Caleb could see Kyle looking at him and smiling, and he
187 felt very lucky to have such a good friend. Ms. Reston then
188 told the class to settle down and to open their math folders.

189 At dinner that evening, Caleb's parents told him that
190 Lucas had been suspended and couldn't come back to
191 school for one week. They also told him that if Lucas ever
192 bullied or threatened another child, he would be expelled,
193 and he would have to go to another school. If Lucas tried
194 to take money from a child again, he would be reported to
195 the police. Then Caleb's parents said that Lucas's father
196 would give back all of the money that Lucas took from
197 Caleb and from Max and Ryan. Caleb would be allowed to
198 keep some of the money to buy a new toy. The rest would
199 go into his bank account.

200 Caleb was so happy, he felt he could almost fly. A great
201 weight had been lifted from his shoulders. He didn't need
202 to be frightened anymore, and he could finally go to
203 recess and have fun. And the best part was that he would
204 be able to have milk with his lunch again!

ORAL QUESTIONS

■ Why do you think Caleb was unwilling to tell the teacher or his parents about Lucas?

Function: *Developing analytical and critical thinking skills.*

Comments: The types of responses you're looking for include:*

- He was afraid to make Lucas mad.
- He was afraid that Lucas would hurt him if he told.
- He was afraid that the teacher wouldn't believe him.
- He was too frightened to think clearly and make the right choices.
- He didn't want to be a cry baby.
- He was afraid that the other children would think less of him if he tattled.

*As previously noted in other units, you don't need to elicit all of these reasons. Be prepared for off-target or illogical responses. These should be treated with sensitivity. As students participate in these class discussions, their reasoning and analytical thinking skills will improve. You want to create a safe context in which students feel that they can freely express their ideas and feelings.

■ What words would you use to describe Caleb? Explain why you've chosen these words.

Function: *Developing observational skills, perceptiveness, empathy, and analytical thinking skills.*

Comments: The types of responses you're looking for include:

- Scared
- Small
- Weak
- Unable to stand up for himself
- Unsure of himself
- Unable to make good decisions

■ How would a child who is being bullied feel?

Function: *Developing analytical thinking skills, evaluative skills, and empathy.*

Comments: The types of responses you are looking for include:

- Sad
- Frightened
- Angry

- Frustrated
- Unhappy
- Afraid to go to school
- Afraid to tell anyone
- Unable to concentrate in school

■ Why didn't Caleb want Kyle to help him?

Function: *Developing analytical thinking skills.*

Comments: The types of responses you're looking for include:

- He was afraid that Kyle wouldn't really be able to protect him.
- He was afraid that if Kyle hit Lucas, things would get worse.
- He didn't want to make Lucas mad.
- He didn't want Kyle to tell the teacher or his parents about what was happening.
- He was ashamed to accept Kyle's help.
- He was hoping that Lucas would decide to stop bullying him.

■ Why do you think Kyle agreed not to say anything to the teacher or his parents?

Function: *Developing analytical thinking skills and empathy.*

Comments: The types of responses you're looking for include:

- He didn't want to upset Caleb.
- Caleb asked him to promise not to say anything.
- He wasn't sure that the teacher or his parents could help.
- He was afraid that he might make things worse.
- He thought that Lucas might stop bullying after he stood up to him at recess.
- He thought that he could handle the situation himself by threatening to beat up Lucas.

■ Is there anything Caleb might have done to deal with his problem?

Function: *Developing analytical, critical, and strategic thinking skills and insight and learning to brainstorm and problem solve. (You may want to use the brainstorming tree on page 12.)*

Comments: The types of responses you're looking for include:

- He could have told his parents about what Lucas was doing.
- He could have told his teacher.

> - He could have stood up to Lucas and punched him in the nose.
> - He could have let his friend Kyle tell the teacher or his parents.
> - He could have asked Kyle to stand up to Lucas every time Lucas threatened him.
> - He could have asked other friends to report what was happening.

■ Why do you think that Kyle felt bad?

> **Function: *Developing analytical and critical thinking skills, insight, and empathy.***
>
> **Comments:** The types of responses you're looking for include:
>
> - He knew that bullying was wrong.
> - Caleb was his friend, and Kyle cared about him.
> - He wanted to protect his friend from Lucas.
> - He felt that he should tell someone, even though he had promised Caleb he wouldn't.
> - He was convinced that Caleb was making a mistake by not telling anyone.
> - He felt that Lucas needed to be stopped.
> - He felt frustrated and powerless to help his friend.
> - He was struggling with whether to break his promise and tell an adult.

■ If your friend makes you promise to keep a secret and you know it would be wrong to do so, what could you do?

> **Function: *Enhancing analytical and critical thinking skills.***
>
> **Comments:** The types of responses you're looking for include:
>
> - I could tell my friend that I can't keep the promise because it would be wrong.
> - I could explain to my friend that I have to do what feels right even if this makes him angry.
> - I could explain to friend why I believe he's making a mistake.
> - I could try to persuade my friend to let me break the promise.
> - I could tell my friend that it's not fair to expect me to keep quiet about something that could cause a serious problem for him or for me.
> - I could explain that the best way to handle the situation is to bring it out into the open.

■ When would you break a promise to a friend?

> **Function: *Enhancing analytical and critical thinking skills.***
>
> **Comments:** The types of responses you're looking for include:
>
> - If my friend could be hurt.
> - If someone else could be hurt.
> - If my friend could get into trouble.
> - If I could get into trouble.
> - If my parents would get very angry or be disappointed in me if I didn't tell.
> - If my teacher would get very angry at me or disappointed in me for not doing what's right.

■ Why do you think children bully other children?

> **Function: *Enhancing analytical and critical thinking skills.***
>
> **Comments:** The types of responses you are looking for include:
>
> - Their parents may not have taught them that bullying is wrong.
> - They enjoy being mean to other kids.
> - They enjoy bossing other kids around.
> - They don't have any friends.
> - They use bullying to get what they want.
> - They believe that they can get away with being cruel.
> - They don't care about hurting other people.
> - They like to make kids afraid of them.
> - They're angry.

■ Is there anything you could do if you saw a child bullying another child?

> **Function: *Developing analytical thinking skills, strategic thinking skills, and empathy.***
>
> **Comments:** The types of responses you are looking for include:
>
> - I could tell the bully to stop.
> - I could refuse to have anything to do with the bully.
> - I could report the bully to the teacher.
> - I could tell my parents.
> - I could tell the bully that other children don't like him because of what he's doing.
> - I could tell the bully that I would be willing to be his friend if he stops being mean.

■ What could happen if a child continues to bully other children?

> **Function:** *Developing analytical, evaluative, and critical thinking skills.*
>
> **Comments:** The types of responses you're looking for include:
>
> - He would lose his friends.
> - He could hurt a child.
> - He would make his parents angry if they find out what he's doing.
> - He would make his teacher angry if she finds out what he's doing.
> - He would get into trouble.
> - He would be punished.
> - He could be suspended from school.
> - He could be expelled from school.
> - He could be arrested by the police.
> - He could be a bully throughout his life.

OPTIONAL ACTIVITY: CAREFUL READING AND ANALYSIS OF THE STORY

(These exercises are designed for students who can read at the second-grade level and above.)

- In the story, certain things happened when Caleb went out to recess. Go back and find the words that describe the four things that Lucas did after he came up to Caleb on the playground. Underline each of these things once and number them in order. (Hint: You can find the description of what Lucas did in lines 11 to 16.)
- The story describes three things that would happen if Caleb tried to hide his milk money from Lucas. Find the words that describe what would happen. Underline each of these three things and number them in order. Then underline two times what Caleb decided about trying to hide his milk money. (Hint: You can find the description of what would happen and Caleb's decision in lines 17 to 27.)
- Lucas told Caleb what to say to the teacher if she asked why he never bought milk in the cafeteria. Find and underline the sentence that describes what Lucas told Caleb to say. (Hint: You can find the sentence in lines 46 to 50.)
- The following day, Kyle saw Lucas taking Caleb's milk money during recess. Find and underline the sentence that describes what Kyle did. (Hint: You can find the two sentences in lines 62 to 67.)
- Kyle tried to protect Caleb, but his friend was upset by what Kyle did to help him. Find and underline how Caleb reacted to what Kyle said to Lucas. (Hint: You can find the sentence in lines 72 to 73.)
- Caleb was very frightened by Lucas, but he didn't want Kyle to help him. Find the words that describe the promise Caleb asked Kyle to make. (Hint: You can find the words in lines 75 to 78.)
- Kyle was tempted to do two things because Caleb was his friend and because it made him sad that Caleb was being bullied by Lucas. Find and underline the two things that Kyle was tempted to do. (Hint: You can find the sentences in lines 81 to 85.)
- When Caleb's parents wanted to talk with him after the parent-teacher conference, Caleb was concerned that his teacher might have said something about his schoolwork. Underline the sentence that describes his concern. (Hint: You can find the sentence in lines 118 to 120.)
- After Caleb's parents found out what Lucas had been doing, his mother made Caleb a promise. Find the sentence that tells about the promise and underline it. (Hint: You can find the sentence in lines 156 to 157.)
- At the end of the story, Caleb's parents describe how Lucas was punished. Find and underline the sentence that describes the punishment. (Hint: You can find the sentence in lines 189 to 191.)
- Caleb's parents also describe three things that would happen if Lucas ever bullied, threatened, or took money from another child. Underline two times the three things that would happen to Lucas. (Hint: You can find the sentences in lines 189 to 195.)

- Underline the sentences that describe what would happen with the money that Lucas took from Caleb. (Hint: Three things would happen, and you can find the sentences in lines 195 to 199.)

SUPPLEMENTAL REPRODUCIBLE EXERCISES

(These supplemental reinforcement exercises can be completed in class or assigned for homework.)

❑ **If you saw a child deliberately hurting another child, what could you do to stop it from happening? Write your ideas in the space below.**

1. _____

2. _____

3. _____

4. _____

❑ **Rate Caleb's decision not to tell the teacher about Lucas.**

Using a Scale:

If you've forgotten how to use a scale to rate something, look back on page 25.

Choose the number that best describes Caleb's decision not to report Lucas to the teacher.

1	2	3	4	5	6	7	8	9	10
Poor				Average					Excellent

❑ **Why did you choose the number that you circled?**

_____

_____

_____

❑ **Rate Caleb's decision not to tell his parents about Lucas.**

Choose the number that best describes Caleb's decision not to say anything to his parents.

1	2	3	4	5	6	7	8	9	10
Poor				Average					Excellent

❑ **Why did you choose the number you circled?**

_____

_____

_____

❑ **Rate the way the principal dealt with Lucas.**

Choose the number that best describes the principal's punishment.

1	2	3	4	5	6	7	8	9	10
Poor				Average					Excellent

❑ **Why did you choose the number that you circled?**

_____

_____

_____

❑ **Do you think that Lucas will continue to bully other children? Yes   No**

If you answered "yes," explain your reasons in the space below.

_____

_____

_____

If you answered "no," explain your reasons in the space below.

_____

_____

_____

❑ **Would you feel guilty about reporting someone who is bullying other children? Yes   No**

If you answered "yes," explain your reasons for feeling guilty in the space below.

_____

_____

_____

If you answered "no," explain your reasons for not feeling guilty in the space below.

_____

_____

_____

❑ **Would you be willing to break a promise if you later decided that keeping the promise was wrong?   Yes   No**

If you answered "yes," explain your reasons in the space below.

_____

_____

_____

If you answered "no," explain your reasons in the space below.

_____

_____

_____

❑ **List reasons why punishing a child for bullying other children might be good for the bully who is being punished.**

1. _____

2. _____

3. _____

❑ **Would you be willing to be friends with a child who stops being a bully? Yes   No**

If you answered "yes," explain your reasons in the space below.

_____

_____

_____

If you answered "no," explain your reasons in the space below.

_____

_____

_____

FOLLOW-UP AND APPLICATION

Despite having extensively examined the issue of bullying with your students, you may not necessarily see immediate behavioral changes in children who are menacing other students. Negative conduct patterns can be difficult to break, and some youngsters may persist in resorting to cruel behavior despite your best efforts to reorient them. This is especially true when the behavior is directly linked to intense underlying feelings of inadequacy and anger.

As noted in previous units, follow-up and reinforcement are critical components in the process of achieving meaningful behavioral change. In a nonpreachy way, you must remind students about the importance of being kind. Those who bully other children must be immediately alerted, cautioned, reprimanded, and punished when you become aware of their behavior. Be prepared for denials. For this reason, it's important to have personally verified that the bullying occurred or to have corroboration if a child reports that another child is bullying.

Students must be periodically reminded that there are not-to-be-violated conduct rules and that there are significant consequences for breaking these rules. These consequences might include calling the child's parents, having a conference with the child's parents, or, if there is another incident of bullying, referring the child to the principal, school counselor, or the school district psychologist or social worker. Bullying is a critically important issue that must be addressed before the behavior causes serious emotional or physical damage to those who are being victimized. In cases in which the bully's conduct is intransigent, intervention by a mental health professional is vital.

At the same time, you must privately acknowledge and affirm students who are making positive changes in their conduct. Let them know that you are aware that they are no longing bullying other children and that you are pleased and proud of them.

CONCRETE REINFORCEMENTS

You might have children break up into small groups and have each group create some simple posters. One might state, "Never be cruel to others." Another might list the consequences of bullying: not having friends, upsetting the teacher, making parents angry, and being punished. These posters will serve as tangible reminders of the issues examined in the unit. You could affix the posters to a wall and periodically have the entire class read one or more of the posters aloud in unison. This reinforcement procedure is an essential element in the cognitive behavioral change process (see page xii). When students are tempted to victimize other students, you want them to have imprinted negative associations with being cruel and menacing.

The objective of these reinforcement activities is for your students to understand unequivocally why bullying is wrong and why it won't be tolerated. Children who bully must be made fully aware of the impact of their behavior.

As a further reinforcement, you could have students do skits that recap what they've discussed. For example, a child playing the role of the bully (definitely not a student who has actually been bullying other children) would intimidate another child. The child might demand lunch money from his victim. The teacher may see what's happening, reprimand the child, and send him to the principal's office. The bully's parents would be called to the principal's office, and the bully would then be sent home. The other children might clap their hands when they find out the bullying has stopped.

Enhancing your students' awareness of unbreakable rules and the consequences for violating the rules is a critically important step in preparing them to deal successfully with society's covenants. Children, both the perpetrators and the victims, must understand that society is intolerant of cruelty.

Children can be taught not to bully, assuming that they don't have serious psychological problems, the cognitive behavioral change instructional process begins early, and the instructional methods are fundamentally sound and consistently applied. Strengthening students' awareness of society's values and strictures, attuning them to fundamental cause-and-effect principles, and improving their analytical, strategic thinking, and problem-solving skills are eminently attainable objectives. By means of effective instruction, guidance, and mentoring, you can, in most cases, head bullying off at the pass, and the impact of your efforts on the life of the bully and the lives of his or her victims will be profound and lasting.

Unit 6

The Child Who Does Poorly in Sports

For Educators

*Examining the Implications
of Being Poorly Coordinated*

Students have different yardsticks by which they measure themselves and assess their abilities and self-worth. Academic achievement, popularity, and athletic abilities are among the most common of these yardsticks. Children who excel in one or more of these venues are more likely to feel accomplished and self-confident than those who are deficient. Achievement furnishes students with tangible evidence of their capabilities and plays a key role in the development of their self-identity. Children may perceive themselves as good readers, math whizzes, computer game luminaries, baseball superstars, karate experts, or soccer champs. Those who are successful in the classroom, shine on the playground, are respected by their peers, and have lots of friends are clearly at the pinnacle of the elementary school hierarchy. They ostensibly "have it all."

Most children—and particularly boys—are keenly aware of their athletic abilities. They are cognizant of how fast they can run, how many push-ups and pull-ups they can do, how well they can dribble and shoot, and how far they can throw or kick a ball. On either a conscious or unconscious level, they recognize how their athletic skills compare with those of their classmates, and the results of this comparison can have a profound impact on their evolving self-concept.

Certainly, athleticism is not the only benchmark of success in elementary school. Children with poor athletic skills may have other talents that distinguish them, provide evidence of their capabilities, and contribute to their self-concept. Youngsters who experience difficulty in PE may one day become highly accomplished, self-assured adults who are titans of industry, megastar singers and musicians, gifted software developers, masterful engineers, highly skilled surgeons, or brilliant astrophysicists. Other poorly coordinated children may not achieve this preeminence, but they may become highly proficient and successful in their chosen careers and vocations. These subsequent achievements, however, may not fully annul the hurt, embarrassment, and humiliation they experienced as children if they were belittled because of their athletic shortcomings. This imprinted pain may still throb years later.

THE ETHOS OF SPORTS

We live in a society that clearly extols sports and sports heroes, and it should not surprise us that children often end up revering athletic prowess. The elevated standing generally afforded students who have superior bodily/ kinesthetic intelligence becomes even more evident in middle school and high school. (See the discussion of bodily/kinesthetic intelligence on pages 35–36.) Top athletes are admired and venerated by their peers. They are invited to the most desirable parties. They date the most popular students. They enjoy influence and status. The star quarterback on the varsity football team and the star power forward on the basketball team often occupy the top rungs on the social-standing ladder. In many schools, being named captain of the hockey, baseball, softball, track, gymnastics, or soccer team furnishes prestige that may eclipse that of even the student body president or the class valedictorian.

Good athletes typically bond together, drawn to each other by shared interests and kindred abilities. These athletes share the rigors of practice, the elation of winning, and the devastating impact of losing. They delight in competing and in testing themselves. Realizing that superior athletes can hit the winning home run, make the difficult catch, sink the tricky shot, and score the tough goal, other children are delighted when these superstars are on their team.

Talented athletes are usually the first selected when sides are chosen in PE or during recess, and they are frequently appointed team captains. Blessed with excellent coordination, they catch, throw, kick, and hit with a fluid grace and ease that's complemented by exceptional eye-hand-foot coordination. The natural athletic abilities and self-confidence of these children often become evident in first grade, and their skills in dodgeball, baseball, soccer, and basketball typically play a key role in enhancing their reputation and popularity.

THE CONSEQUENCES OF POOR COORDINATION

Students with poor coordination and skills are obviously at a distinct disadvantage during recess and PE. Not only are they at the lower end of the athletic performance continuum, they are also frequently at the lower end of the social-standing continuum. Their deficiencies when playing sports produce diminished athletic self-confidence that, in turn, often results in diminished social self-confidence. Acutely aware of their physical limitations, these youngsters usually dread PE. They repeatedly miss catchable popup flies and easy grounders when playing baseball or softball. They frequently strike out when they bat. They rarely hit the backboard with a basketball, much less the rim, and when they kick a soccer ball or kickball, it seldom travels more than a few feet. Their movements are awkward and disjointed, and they often stumble, trip, and fall when playing sports. Because their motor skills and eye-hand and eye-foot coordination are deficient, they frequently misjudge where the ball is going. They are among the first to be eliminated or benched during a game, and they are the last to be selected when sides are chosen. Those who venture to play Little League generally spend most of their time sitting on the bench.

They're usually assigned to bat at the end of the order, and their coaches reluctantly insert them in the outfield only because league regulations require that children play a minimum number of innings. Perceived as a liability by their teammates, these nonperformers quickly become resigned to their athletic incompetence.

Most poor athletes will consciously or unconsciously try to compensate for their coordination deficiencies and athletic ineptitude. If their compensatory mechanisms are strategic and effectual, they'll orient toward other pursuits in which they have talent. They may gravitate toward art, acting, chess, or computers. They may focus their energies on achieving academically, earning merit badges in Cub Scouts or Brownies, doing art, or building projects. Because of their capabilities in other areas, these nonathletic children may develop a very positive sense of self. Nonetheless, their struggles on the playground, in the gym, and on the playing field are still likely to have a negative emotional impact, especially if they're teased and demeaned because of their subpar skills.

Of far greater concern are poor athletes who either do not possess other demonstrable abilities or who haven't yet discovered their natural talents. These students are at psychological risk, especially if other children repeatedly disparage them for their failings. If their compensatory behavior is ineffectual, they're likely to become increasingly demoralized, and they're apt to express their frustration and feelings of incompetence either by acting out or by withdrawing into a shell. When children's defense mechanisms are particularly maladaptive, inappropriate, and off-putting, their behavior can lead to social rejection and alienation. During a game, athletically inept children may act silly or goofy or make fun of themselves. Despite their attempts to make light of their coordination deficits, these children ache inside. They desperately want to be able to play sports with at least a modicum of ability. They desperately want to be accepted and respected by their classmates. And they desperately want to avoid being disparaged by their teammates.

When children's poor athletic skills repeatedly cause their team to lose games, they are especially vulnerable to being ridiculed by their peers. Their chronic errors and miscues may cause their teammates to groan, laugh, and make hurtful comments. Acutely aware that they are letting their teammates down, these children usually begin to see themselves as albatrosses.

For students who are very poorly coordinated, participating in PE is usually a nightmare and something to be avoided if at all possible. Some children may feign a sore throat, headache, or stomachache to secure a note from their parents requesting that they be excused them from having to go to PE. To youngsters who are emotionally vulnerable, the fight-or-flight dilemma is a no-brainer. Whenever possible, their self-protecting instincts will make flight the more desirable option. As previously stated, the negative associations that these athletically inept children have with sports may endure throughout their lives.

ANTIDOTES FOR ATHLETIC INSUFFICIENCIES

Helping poorly coordinated students uncover their natural talents and distinctive intelligence type can play a crucial role in safeguarding their self-esteem.

Significantly more, however, can be done to help children surmount their athletic insufficiencies.

Students with glaring motor coordination deficits can be assigned to adaptive PE classes where specially trained teachers can focus on improving their basic skills in kickball, softball, and basketball. Applying "divide and conquer principles," adaptive PE instructors can break down each sport into its component parts and provide repeated opportunities for athletically challenged students to practice and master each component. Specific drills and exercises can be used to enhance the ability of these children to dribble and shoot a basketball, catch and hit a softball, and kick a soccer ball.

Many school districts also have occupational therapists on staff or under contract who can evaluate poorly coordinated students and, when appropriate, provide specialized therapeutic training when the coordination deficits are chronic and extreme. These licensed occupational therapists have received comprehensive training in methods specifically designed to help children improve their balance, gross- and fine-motor coordination, and eye-hand-foot coordination. These basic competencies are requisites to children being able to participate successfully in school athletic programs, develop a positive body image, and acquire athletic confidence. Within a few months, students can often demonstrably improve their motor skills, and the psychological rewards can be stupendous. Students who previously perceived themselves as hopelessly inadequate in sports may undergo a radical self-concept transformation. These youngsters probably won't become athletic superstars, but they can usually learn how to catch, bat, kick, and dribble to get a ball to go where they want it to go. This skills enhancement is in many respects the equivalent of a "complete athletic makeover."

EXAMINING THE STORY

The student-directed story and the analytical thinking activities in this unit are designed to heighten your students' awareness of the negative impact of disparagement on children who are having difficulty playing sports. The description of the protagonist's behavior and feelings should resonate not only in children who are poorly coordinated but also in children who may be demeaning the athletically challenged child. (*Please note:* To make the following examination of the issues more concrete, you may want to skip ahead and read the story.)

The anecdote describes a poorly coordinated child who detests PE and who is being subjected to disparagement by his classmates. The story describes Jeremy's feelings of hurt, embarrassment, humiliation, and alienation, and at the same time the story affirms that such problems can be fixed, even when the difficulties appear overwhelming and insoluble. An equally important objective is to guide students who are being demeaned because of their athletic deficiencies to the realization that their parents and teachers are their first line of defense against teasing and that they should feel safe confiding in these adults.

The story and the questions that follow the story provide students with an opportunity to examine why some children have trouble playing sports. The anecdote also describes how Jeremy's mother and the school administration respond to Jeremy's problem. Students learn that they have potent allies who will make every effort to help them.

By teaching your students how to confront and solve problems and dilemmas, you're providing them with a tangible and accessible resource that they will be able to use throughout life. You want to guide your students to the realization that most problems in life are solvable if they think strategically.

THE QUESTIONS THAT FOLLOW THE STORY

See Unit 1 (page 10) for suggestions about how you might present the questions to help students carefully examine the story and understand the key issues. The recommended procedural template is essentially the same for all of the units in this program.

For Students

The Child Who Does Poorly in Sports

THE STORY

1 As usual, Jeremy was walking at a snail's pace as he
2 made his way to the playing field. The third grader was in
3 no hurry to find out what sort of terrible activity the PE
4 teacher had planned for the class. Whatever it was,
5 Jeremy was certain that it would make his life miserable.

6 Mr. Rollins, whom the kids called Coach, saw Jeremy
7 lagging behind and yelled at him to hurry up. Jeremy reluc-
8 tantly broke into a very slow trot. He was determined to put
9 off what was about to happen next for as long as possible.

10 When Jeremy arrived at the field, all of the third graders
11 from two classes were standing together in a large group.
12 The coach had already selected two students to be cap-
13 tains of the dodgeball teams, and they had started choos-
14 ing sides. The children who were picked stood next to the
15 captain of their team. About ten children hadn't yet been
16 selected, and Jeremy joined them. These were the worst
17 dodgeball players, and they were always chosen last.

18 As usual, Jeremy was the very last child picked. Some
19 of the kids groaned when they realized that Jeremy had to
20 be on their side. Jeremy's cheeks turned red, and he
21 stared down at the ground, hoping that by doing so he
22 would somehow become invisible. Being picked last was
23 bad enough. Having his teammates make fun of him
24 made it even worse.

25 Of course, Jeremy understood why he was always the
26 last child picked when sides were chosen. He knew that he

was terrible at dodgeball. In fact, he realized that he was terrible at all sports. When he played softball, he would usually strike out. If by some miracle he did hit the ball, it would almost always be a slow roller to the pitcher. When his team took the field, he was always assigned to the outfield. It didn't matter whether he was in right field, center field, or left field, he would misjudge the fly balls and bobble the grounders. Then he would throw the ball twenty feet away from the infielder who was waiting for the relay.

What bothered Jeremy most was when the other kids laughed at him every time he messed up. When this happened, he wished he could somehow magically disappear. He realized he was letting his teammates down, and he knew that everyone was upset with him. If his team lost the game, the kids would usually blame him and call him a bobble head.

It was the same when Jeremy played basketball. He could never control the ball when he was dribbling it down the court. If he took a shot, the ball almost never hit the backboard, much less the rim. In fact, Jeremy had made only one basket all year, and that was purely by accident. Another child was trying to steal the basketball from him, and in desperation, Jeremy threw the ball up into the air in the direction of the basket. Somehow it miraculously went through the hoop. Everyone was so shocked that the game actually stopped while the kids stared at each other and shook their heads in disbelief.

"Good shot!" Coach had yelled.

"I don't believe it! Jeremy got a basket," the boy guarding him shouted.

"Lucky shot," said another player on the opposing team.

It was the same with soccer. When Jeremy tried to kick the ball, he would usually miss it or kick it in the wrong direction. Because he would get bored standing around, he rarely paid attention to the game. Then someone would boot the ball toward him, and everyone would start yelling at him. Jeremy would usually get so upset and confused that he could barely move.

Jeremy gets a lucky basket.

65   Instead of going to PE, Jeremy would have much
66 preferred to go to the school library where he could read
67 about reptiles. This was his favorite topic. His dream was
68 to become a herpetologist, a snake specialist. "Who cares
69 about stupid dodgeball or dumb basketball?" Jeremy
70 thought angrily.

71   When they played dodgeball in PE, Jeremy was the
72 first person that the kids on the other team tried to hit with
73 the ball. He could never move fast enough to avoid being
74 smashed, and he rarely caught any of the balls that were
75 thrown at him. Because he was usually the first child hit,
76 he always ended up behind the line with all of the other
77 kids who were eliminated.

78   As he feared, Coach had decided to have the third
79 graders play dodgeball again. "I hate dodgeball," Jeremy
80 remarked to Jason, his best friend. Both boys had been hit
81 immediately after the game began, and as usual, they were
82 standing in their regular place behind the chalked "out" line.
83 Jeremy looked longingly at the field that bordered the
84 school and thought about all the fun he and Jason could be
85 having looking for garter snakes and lizards.

86   "I hate it, too." Jason replied.

87   Kevin overheard Jeremy and Jason talking. "You two
88 don't like dodgeball because you're terrible at it," Kevin

Jeremy missing the soccer ball.

89 snickered. Jeremy wasn't surprised by the comment.
90 Usually, Kevin never talked to either of them unless he
91 had something nasty to say.

92 Jeremy was shocked that Kevin was behind the line.
93 He was the best dodgeball player in the class, and he
94 usually was the last child still in the game. Somehow a
95 child on the other team had made a lucky throw that
96 caught Kevin by surprise. The ball had glanced off his
97 shoulder, and Kevin was out. Jeremy could tell that Kevin
98 was furious about having to stand behind the line.

99 "You guys are so awful that no one wants you on his
100 team," Kevin continued with a sneer on his face.

101 Jeremy and Jason didn't say anything. Kevin's words
102 cut through them like a sword, and they stared down at
103 the ground.

104 That evening Jeremy helped his mother clear off the
105 table and load the dishwasher. His mom asked him if he
106 had completed his homework, and Jeremy assured her
107 that he had.

108 "Mom, my hip is hurting me again," Jeremy said in a
109 low voice after the last dish had been placed in the dish-
110 washer. "Could you write me a note so that I don't have to
111 go to PE tomorrow?"

112
113
"Jeremy, what's going on? This is the second time this week that you've asked me to write a note for you."

114
"My hip really, really hurts!" Jeremy insisted.

115
116
"Well, I don't see you limping. Do I need to make an appointment with Dr. Ross?"

117
"No," Jeremy replied.

118
"What's really happening, Jeremy?"

119
120
At first, Jeremy didn't say anything. His mother turned and looked at him.

121
"OK, what is it, son?" she asked gently.

122
123
A tear rolled down Jeremy's cheek, and he just looked down at the floor.

124
125
"Jeremy, I can't help you with the problem if you don't tell me what the problem is."

126
127
128
"Mom, I'm really awful at PE. I'm always picked last, and the kids make fun of me," Jeremy sobbed. "They call me a bobble head."

129
130
"Does the PE teacher let them make fun of you?" his mother asked in a concerned voice.

131
132
133
134
135
"He tells them to stop, but sometimes he can't hear what they're saying. I feel terrible because I usually make my team lose the game. The kids tease me during recess, and they tell me that they don't want me to play on their team."

136
137
138
139
"It makes me very sad that children are making fun of you. I think we need to discuss this situation with the vice principal," Jeremy's mother said as she gently stroked his head.

140
141
"I just want to go to the library and read instead of having to go to dumb PE."

142
143
"Honey, exercise is good for you. Kids need to run around and play sports. You can't spend all of your time

144 reading. We need to stop the teasing, and we need to
145 get you some help so that you can do better in sports.
146 Tomorrow, we're going to talk with the vice principal. Just
147 hang in there for now. Wait until we find out what can be
148 done to solve the problem."

149 Jeremy didn't really believe that anything could be
150 done, but he felt better knowing that his mom finally
151 understood why he hated PE. He would wait until tomor-
152 row to find out what the vice principal had to say. He was
153 hoping that Mr. Taneka would just give him permission to
154 go to the library instead of having to go to PE.

155 The next day, Jeremy and his mother went to see
156 the vice principal after school. While his mother spoke
157 with Mr. Taneka, Jeremy waited outside the office. Then
158 Mr. Taneka came to the door and asked him to come in.
159 Jeremy had never been in the vice principal's office, and
160 he was very nervous. Usually kids were sent to the vice
161 principal when they were in trouble.

162 "Jeremy, your mother tells me that some of your class-
163 mates are making fun of you during PE," Mr. Taneka said.
164 "Is this true?"

Jeremy's mom comforts him.

165 "Yes," Jeremy replied in a very low voice.

166 "Does this happen a lot?"

167 "Yes," Jeremy again replied in a very low voice.

168 "I can understand why being made fun of would make
169 you sad and make you not want to go to PE," Mr. Taneka
170 said in very serious voice.

171 Jeremy didn't say anything. He just stared down at his
172 hand. Tears began to roll down his cheeks.

173 "Nobody likes to be teased, Jeremy, and it upsets
174 me that this is happening in our school. I promise you that
175 the nasty remarks will stop. I will ask Mr. Rollins to remind
176 the students about the school rules about making fun of
177 other children, and I will ask him to make certain that the
178 children obey these rules. I'm also going to have you visit
179 with a special teacher we have here. Her name is Ms. Kim,
180 and she's an occupational therapist. She does special
181 exercises and activities with children to help them improve
182 their coordination and balance so that they can do better
183 in sports. She may also recommend that you go to a dif-
184 ferent PE class. It's called adaptive PE, and the teacher in
185 this class would work with you on improving your base-
186 ball, basketball, and soccer skills. Does this plan sound
187 OK to you?"

188 "Yes," Jeremy replied softly. He didn't know what else to
189 say.

190 "Other students have also had difficulty playing sports,
191 and after working with Ms. Kim, they all made wonderful
192 improvement. I'm certain you will, too, Jeremy. OK?"

193 "OK," Jeremy answered, but his voice didn't sound as
194 if he was very convinced.

195 Mr. Taneka said he wanted to talk more with Jeremy's
196 mom, and he asked Jeremy to wait in the outer office. As
197 Jeremy was leaving, he looked at his mom, and she
198 smiled at him.

199   That evening, Jeremy told his mother that Mr. Rollins
200 had talked to the class about teasing. He had been very
201 stern. He told the children that he would send them to
202 Mr. Taneka's office if he ever heard anyone making fun of
203 another student during PE. He also told the students to
204 report any teasing on the playground, in the lunchroom, or
205 after school.

206   "That's great, Jeremy!" his mom said with a big smile
207 on her face. "Does this make you feel any better?"

208   "A little," Jeremy replied. "But I know what they're think-
209 ing even if they don't say anything mean. They still think
210 I'm a bobble head, and they don't want me on their team."

211   "Well, the first step in dealing with the problem was to
212 stop the teasing. The next step is to help you improve your
213 athletic skills. I filled out the paperwork for you to be tested
214 by Ms. Kim. You'll see her next Tuesday during your regu-
215 lar PE class. She'll have you do some exercises and activ-
216 ities so that she can develop a plan to improve your skills."

217   Jeremy felt a little better, but he wasn't sure that doing
218 exercises with Ms. Kim would really help him in dodgeball
219 or baseball. Well, he would just wait and see. At least one
220 good thing was going to happen. He wouldn't have to go
221 to PE next Tuesday.

222   Jeremy didn't really think he'd actually be able to do
223 better in sports, but it turned out to be true. Six months
224 later, he was back in his regular PE class, and he was hit-
225 ting, fielding, batting, and kicking like a champ!

ORAL QUESTIONS

■ Why do you think Jeremy would always walk slowly to the playing field when it was time to go to PE?

Function: *Developing analytical and critical thinking skills and empathy.*

Comments: The types of responses you're looking for include:*

- He hated PE.
- He wanted to put off PE for as long as possible.
- He knew that he would play poorly.
- He was embarrassed that he played sports poorly.
- He was afraid that he would probably cause his team to lose.
- He didn't want to be teased.
- He wasn't interested in playing sports.

*As previously noted in other units, you don't need to elicit all of these reasons. Be prepared for off-target or illogical responses. These should be treated with sensitivity. As students participate in these class discussions, their reasoning and analytical thinking skills will improve. You want to create a safe context in which students feel that they can freely express their ideas and feelings.

■ What words would you use to describe Jeremy? Explain why you've chosen these words.

Function: *Developing observational skills, perceptiveness, empathy, and analytical thinking skills.*

Comments: The types of responses you're looking for include:

- Sad
- Unsure of himself
- Bad at sports
- Embarrassed
- Ashamed
- Unpopular
- Frustrated
- Discouraged
- Angry

■ Why do you think Jeremy didn't say something to Coach about the kids making fun of him?

Function: *Developing analytical thinking skills, evaluative skills, and empathy.*

Comments: The types of responses you're looking for include:

- He was afraid that the other children would think he was a crybaby.

- He didn't want the other children to get angry at him.
- He believed that if he complained, things would get worse.
- He didn't think the coach would do anything to help him with the problem.
- He was embarrassed.
- He was ashamed to talk about his problem.
- He was hoping that his mom would do something to get him excused from PE.

■ Why do you think Jeremy didn't say anything to his mother about the teasing?

Function: _Developing analytical thinking skills._

Comments: The types of responses you're looking for include:

- He was afraid that she wouldn't understand.
- He felt that she might blame him for the problem.
- He thought she might tell him just to try harder.
- He thought she might say something to Coach that would embarrass him even more.
- He was afraid that she would ask for the names of the children who were making fun of him and call their parents.
- He was afraid things would get worse if his mother called the parents of the children who were teasing him.

■ Why do you think that the vice principal wanted Jeremy to see Ms. Kim and maybe go into a different PE class?

Function: _Developing analytical thinking skills._

Comments: The types of responses you are looking for include:

- He wanted to help Jeremy with his problem.
- He didn't want Jeremy to be sad.
- He didn't want Jeremy to be embarrassed or frustrated.
- He didn't want Jeremy to be teased if he caused his team to loose.
- He thought that Ms. Kim could help Jeremy play better.
- He thought that the special PE class could help Jeremy improve in sports and learn how to hit, catch, shoot, dribble, and kick better.
- He thought Jeremy would be happier in another PE class.
- The kids in the other PE class wouldn't tease him because they also were having difficulty in sports.

■ Is there anything Jeremy could have done on his own to deal with his problem?

Function: *Developing analytical and critical thinking skills and insight and learning to brainstorm and problem solve. (You may want to use the brainstorming tree on page 12.)*

Comments: The types of responses you're looking for include:

- He could have asked the coach to help him learn how to play better.
- He and his friend Jason could have practiced throwing, catching, hitting, and kicking.
- He could have asked a child who was good at sports to help him.
- He could have asked his mom or dad to play catch and basketball with him.
- He could have asked the kids not to make fun of him.
- He could have reported the teasing to his teacher or his coach.

■ Why do you think that the other kids made fun to Jeremy?

Function: *Developing analytical and critical thinking skills, insight, and empathy.*

Comments: The types of responses you're looking for include:

- He made errors when he played sports.
- He often caused his team to lose the game.
- He looked funny when he played sports.
- He didn't like doing what other kids liked doing.
- He didn't stand up for himself.
- The other kids thought Jeremy's interest in snakes was weird.
- The other kids didn't like him because he acted differently than they did.

■ Why do kids think sports are so important?

Function: *Enhancing analytical and critical thinking skills.*

Comments: The types of responses you're looking for include:

- Sports are fun to play.
- Kids watch college and professional teams on TV with their parents.
- Kids go to high school games with their older brothers and sisters.
- Kids like to have favorite teams.
- Kids like to be on Little League, basketball, and soccer teams.
- It's fun to play sports in PE and after school.
- PE is a nice break from being in class and working hard.
- Kids like to win games and to be good at sports.
- Kids like to look up to their favorite sports heroes.

■ Why do you think children tease others?

> **Function: *Enhancing analytical and critical thinking skills.***
>
> **Comments:** The types of responses you're looking for include:
>
> - Their parents may not have taught them that it's wrong to tease.
> - They like being mean.
> - They don't respect kids who can't do what they can do.
> - They don't think that teasing is hurting other children.
> - They don't care about hurting other children.
> - They think they can get away with being mean.
> - They think that if they tease, other kids will think they're cool.

■ Is there anything you could do to help a child who is doing poorly in sports?

> **Function: *Enhancing analytical and critical thinking skills, empathy, and compassion.***
>
> **Comments:** The types of responses you're looking for include:
>
> - I could practice playing with him.
> - I could be his friend.
> - I could give him suggestions about how to play better.
> - I could pick him to play on my team if I were the captain.
> - I could tell other children not to make fun of him.
> - I could tell the teacher if someone is teasing him.

■ What should happen to children who continue to make fun of other children?

> **Function: *Developing analytical thinking skills, strategic thinking skills, and empathy.***
>
> **Comments:** The types of responses you're looking for include:
>
> - They should be reported to the teacher.
> - They should not be permitted to go to recess.
> - They should be kept after school.
> - They should be sent to the vice principal's office.
> - They should not be allowed to play sports during PE.
> - They should be helped to understand why teasing is wrong.
> - The other kids should refuse to be their friends if they continue teasing.

OPTIONAL ACTIVITY: CAREFUL READING AND ANALYSIS OF THE STORY

(These exercises are designed for students who can read at the second-grade level and above.)

- The story tells about Jeremy's difficulties in softball, basketball, soccer, and dodgeball. Find the words that describe his difficulties in each of these sports. Underline each sport two times, and then underline once each difficulty that he had in that sport. Then number each difficulty in order. (Hint: The descriptions are found in lines 28 to 77.) For example, you should be able to find four problems he had when he played softball. You should be able to find two problems he had when he played basketball. You should be able to find three problems when he played soccer and three problems when he played dodgeball.

- When Jeremy's teammates laughed at him for messing up in softball, he felt like he wanted to disappear. Find and underline the three reasons why playing poorly made him feel bad. (Hint: You can find the reasons in lines 36 to 42.)

- Jeremy had difficulty playing basketball, but he actually got one basket. Find and underline the words that describe how this happened. (Hint: You can find the description of how Jeremy scored the basket in lines 46 to 51.)

- Find and underline the sentence that describes what Jeremy would prefer to be doing with his friend Jason instead of having to play dodgeball. (Hint: You can find the sentence in lines 83 to 85.)

- The story describes two mean things that Kevin said to Jeremy and Jason during the dodgeball game. Go back and find the two mean statements, and underline each statement one time. (Hint: You can find what Kevin said in lines 87 to 100.)

- Find and underline what Jeremy said to his mom about what was wrong with him. Then find and underline what he asked his mother to do. (Hint: You can find the sentences in lines 108 to 111.)

- The vice principal promised to do something about the children who were making fun of Jeremy. Find and underline the two things that Mr. Taneka said he would tell Mr. Rollins. (Hint: You can find the sentence in lines 175 to 178.)

- Mr. Taneka had a plan for helping Jeremy improve in sports. Find and underline what he was going to do. (Hint: His plan involved Ms. Kim. You can find the sentences in lines 178 to 180.)

- Find and underline the words that describe how Ms. Kim helps students do better in sports. (Hint: You can find the sentence in lines 180 to 183.)

- Find and underline the words that describe what Mr. Rollins warned would happen if students made fun of other students in PE class, on the playground, in the lunchroom, or after school. (Hint: You can find the sentence in lines 201 to 203.)

- Jeremy didn't really believe that Mr. Taneka's plan would work. Find, underline one time, and number what actually happened. (Hint: You can find the sentence at the very end of the story in lines 223 to 225.)

SUPPLEMENTAL REPRODUCIBLE EXERCISES

(These supplemental reinforcement exercises can be completed in class or assigned for homework.)

❏ **If someone was making fun of or teasing another child because he had difficulty in sports, what could you do to stop it from happening? Write your ideas in the space below.**

1. _____

2. _____

3. _____

4. _____

❏ **Rate the decision made by Jeremy's mother to discuss the problem with the vice principal.**

Using a Scale

If you've forgotten how to use a scale to rate something, look back on page 25.

Choose the number that best describes the decision to talk with the vice principal.

1	2	3	4	5	6	7	8	9	10
Poor				Average					Excellent

❏ **Why did you choose the number that you circled?**

_____

_____

_____

❏ **Rate Mr. Taneka's ideas for dealing with Jeremy's problem.**

Choose the number that best describes Mr. Taneka's ideas.

1	2	3	4	5	6	7	8	9	10
Poor				Average					Excellent

❏ **Why did you choose the number that you circled?**

_____

_____

_____

❏ **Rate how successful the plan for improving Jeremy's athletic skills will be.**

Choose the number that best describes how successful you think the plan will be.

1	2	3	4	5	6	7	8	9	10
No Success			Average Success				Great Success		

❏ **Why did you choose the number that you circled?**

_____

_____

_____

❏ **Coach warned the students about making fun of children who are struggling. Rate how successful you think his warning about teasing will be in changing the students' behavior.**

Choose the number that best describes what you think about the effectiveness of the coach's warning.

1	2	3	4	5	6	7	8	9	10
No Success			Average Success				Great Success		

❏ **Why did you choose the number that you circled?**

_____

_____

_____

❏ **Do you think that the third graders at Jeremy's school will stop making fun of children who are struggling in PE?   Yes   No**

If you answered "yes," explain your reasons in the space below.

_____

_____

_____

If you answered "no," explain your reasons in the space below.

_____

_____

_____

❏ **Would you feel guilty about reporting someone who is teasing other children?   Yes   No**

If you answered "yes," explain your reasons for feeling guilty in the space below.

_____

_____

_____

If you answered "no," explain your reasons for not feeling guilty in the space below.

_____

_____

_____

❏ **List reasons why punishing a child who teases another child might be good for the child who is being punished.**

1. _____

2. _____

3. _____

❑ **Would you be willing to be friends with a child who is not good in sports?   Yes   No**

If you answered "yes," explain your reasons in the space below.

_____

_____

_____

If you answered "no," explain your reasons in the space below.

_____

_____

_____

❑ **Would you be willing to help a child who is not good in sports learn how to play better?   Yes   No**

If you answered "yes," explain your reasons in the space below.

_____

_____

_____

If you answered "no," explain your reasons in the space below.

_____

_____

_____

FOLLOW-UP AND APPLICATION

Despite having examined with your students the plight of children who have difficulty playing sports, you may not necessarily see immediate changes in the behavior of students who are intolerant of and disparaging toward those with poor athletic abilities. As previously noted in other units, negative conduct patterns can be difficult to break, and some students may continue to be highly critical of their classmates despite your best efforts to reorient their behavior. The desire to be on a winning team can be consuming, and children who are intent on victory may find it difficult to demonstrate empathy and compassion for those who cause their team to lose.

Follow-up, reinforcement, and consistency are critical components in the process of achieving meaningful behavioral change. In a nonpreachy way, you should remind students about the importance of being kind. Those who deprecate other children must be immediately alerted, cautioned, reminded, and, if appropriate, reprimanded when you become aware of their intolerant behavior. Be prepared for denials. For this reason, it's important to have personally witnessed the disparagement or to have corroboration if a child reports that another child is being cruel and belittling.

Students must be periodically reminded that there are rules of socially acceptable behavior and that there are consequences for breaking these rules. These consequences might include calling the child's parents and having a conference with the child's parents. Disparagement is an important issue that must be addressed before the behavior causes emotional damage to those who are being belittled. You should privately acknowledge and affirm students who positively alter their behavior. Let them know that you are aware that they're being more tolerant and that you are pleased and proud of them. At the same time, you want to encourage students in your class who are poor athletes. If you supervise recess or teach PE, you might occasionally appoint these children captains of dodgeball and kickball teams. You'll also want to acknowledge and affirm the less talented athletes in your class when they do something well or show that they're making progress. If another person supervises recess or PE, you might want to broach diplomatically some of the concepts examined in this unit. This intercession is especially important if you suspect that the person supervising does not fully recognize or appreciate the psychological damage that is likely to occur when children do poorly in sports and are disparaged by their peers for their athletic deficiencies.

CONCRETE REINFORCEMENTS

You might have children break up into small groups and have each group create some simple posters. One might state, "Don't ever make fun of other children." Another might read, "Be kind to kids who are having difficulty doing something," and a third poster might read, "Encourage children who are struggling." These posters will serve as tangible reminders of the issues that have been examined in the unit. You could affix the posters to a wall and periodically have the entire class read one or more of the posters aloud in unison. This reinforcement procedure is a critically important component in the cognitive behavioral change instructional model (see page xii).

When students are tempted to belittle other students who are having difficulty in sports—or in any area, for that matter—you want them to recognize that this is cruel behavior that is unacceptable. You also want them to be aware of the impact of this behavior on others. Providing acknowledgment and praise for treating others with kindness is essential to teaching your students to be more compassionate and empathetic.

As a further reinforcement, you could have students do skits that recap what they've discussed. For example, a child (definitely not a student who actually has coordination deficits) could pretend to strike out in softball or miss a pop fly. Some students might laugh and make fun of him. Then other students might tell them to stop because what they're doing is cruel. They might take the poor athlete aside and teach him how to swing the bat better. The poorly coordinated child might then get a hit in the pantomime, and the children would clap their hands and pat him on the back.

Enhancing students' awareness of acceptable codes of behavior is an essential element in preparing them to deal successfully with society's expectations and demands. Children must realize that it's not OK to be intolerant of others who are struggling.

As has been noted in other units, teaching children to be more compassionate is an unequivocally attainable goal, assuming the process begins early enough and the behavioral change instructional procedures are sound and consistently applied. Strengthening your students' awareness of social values, strictures, and cause-and-effect principles and enhancing their analytical, strategic thinking, and problem-solving skills are also unequivocally attainable goals. With effective instruction, guidance, and mentoring, these objectives can be realized in your classroom, and the impact of your efforts on your students' lives will be profound and lasting.

Appendix 1
Psychological Overlay and Learning Differences

Learning problems can obviously be a primary source of children's psychological distress. It should not come as a surprise when children who are confused and unable to do the assigned work often conclude either consciously or unconsciously that they're incompetent. These youngsters are keenly aware that they must continually struggle while their classmates appear able to learn with relatively little effort.

A steady diet of failure, frustration, and discouragement can quickly erode the emotional resources of academically beleaguered students. A basic survival instinct impels these children to protect themselves psychologically. Unfortunately, the common defense mechanisms—laziness, procrastination, irresponsibility, acting out, blaming, denial, and resistance—offer only an illusory protection, and these self-defeating behaviors and attitudes only magnify the learning difficulties of these children. Of course, struggling students who are entangled in their own coping mechanisms rarely perceive this obvious irony.

UNDERSTANDING PSYCHOLOGICAL OVERLAY

The maladaptive conduct of some students with learning differences may appear quite willful to adults. Struggling students, however, do not, in fact, consciously plan how they're going to compensate for their feelings of inadequacy. They don't say to themselves, *"I'm doing poorly in school, and I feel frustrated and demoralized. I think I'll misbehave and slug this kid or talk back to my teacher so that I can let everyone know how unhappy I am."* The behavior is unconsciously driven, and most students are not aware of the scripts they've created to cope with their distress. Some students with learning differences may shut down and refuse to study or complete their assignments. Others may become hostile, disrespectful, resistant, or rebellious. Still others may escape into daydreams or compensate for their academic deficiencies by focusing exclusively on athletics or video games.

The frustration, anger, fear, insecurity, and feelings of incompetence that struggling students often experience may implode and manifest as depression or may explode and manifest as hostility, aggression, antisocial behavior, and, in extreme cases, as a conduct disorder. Between these two extremes are countless possibilities for children to express their pain, resentment, demoralization, sadness, and anger.

Despairing teachers may conclude that struggling students are acting inappropriately to *get attention* when, in fact, these students are actually resorting to these maladaptive behaviors in a misguided attempt to *deflect attention* from their inadequacies and camouflage their feelings of inferiority. If the unconscious mind of the child with learning differences could give voice to the underlying feelings that are driving his or her counterproductive conduct, it would probably say, *"I feel so stupid! If I act this way, maybe you won't see how dumb I am."*

The warning signs of emotional distress may be blatant in some cases and subtle and difficult to identify in others. When the danger signals are subtle, teachers, parents, and even mental health professionals may fail to recognize the red flags. The consequences of this oversight could be calamitous. Problems that might have been quickly resolved in first or second grade are all but certain to become far more challenging to resolve in eighth or ninth grade.

Students with learning differences who receive learning assistance and who can see that they're making progress are far less likely to resort to counterproductive behavior. Conversely, students who are convinced that their academic situation is hopeless and that effort is futile are clearly at risk for becoming increasingly frustrated, demoralized, and psychologically defensive.

IDENTIFYING THE SYMPTOMS OF PSYCHOLOGICAL OVERLAY

Psychological overlay refers to patterns of counterproductive, maladaptive, and self-sabotaging behaviors and attitudes that compound students' learning difficulties. The overlay is a reactive phenomenon. Students with learning problems may be deeply embarrassed when they're asked to read aloud. They may be overwhelmed by catastrophic expectations when they take tests. They may crumble when they receive a poor grade. They may feel humiliated when they cannot answer a question in class or do a math problem at the chalkboard. As they battle to decipher words, follow directions, and understand the content of their textbooks, these children will usually seek to protect themselves psychologically, and their instinctive defense mechanisms typically manifest as psychological overlay. (Children can, of course, also exhibit the symptoms of psychological overlay in reaction to other distressing situations such as social rejection, teasing, poor athletic performance, and bullying.)

School for students with learning differences can be a recurring nightmare. Each day they confront a host of monumental challenges, seemingly insoluble problems, and depressing disappointments. Dreading situations that might expose their inadequacies and subject them to real or imagined ridicule, they often feel compelled to camouflage their deficiencies and compensate for their failings.

Once struggling children conclude that pain and humiliation are inescapable no matter how hard they try, they're at serious risk for shutting down academically. They may ensconce themselves in a comfort zone where they can avoid responsibility. They may become uninvolved and listless. They may act out. They may become class clowns. They may refuse to study and do their homework. They may procrastinate. They may submit incomplete, illegible, and inaccurate assignments and miss deadlines. They may become helpless and dependent on their parents, teachers, and tutors. They may rebel and develop chronic conduct problems. Although these students may continue to go through the mechanical motions of acquiring an education, they have, for all intents and purposes, already given up.

BEHAVIORS AND ATTITUDES THAT MAY INDICATE PSYCHOLOGICAL OVERLAY

- Apathy
- Anxiety
- Manipulative behavior
- Avoidance
- Self-sabotaging behavior
- Passive learning
- Aggression (active or passive)
- Hostility
- Depression
- Helplessness
- Irresponsibility
- Lying
- Immaturity
- Procrastination
- Daydreaming
- Acting out
- Clowning
- Blaming
- Complaining
- Withdrawal
- Reduced motivation
- Denial
- Depression
- Diminished self-confidence
- Feelings of being oppressed
- Lowered expectations and aspirations
- Resistance to studying
- Fear of failure, success, or competition
- Resistance to help
- Resistance to authority
- Profound feelings of incompetence and inadequacy
- Identification with a nonachieving, alienated, rebellious, or antisocial peer group

In many instances, psychological overlay will disappear as children begin to make academic progress and experience success in school. The keys are early intervention and effective remediation before the negative attitudes and behaviors become entrenched.

Students who have been struggling with learning problems for many years and who have been scarred by their negative school experiences are unlikely to relinquish readily their maladaptive behaviors and attitudes. Deeply embedded psychological overlay may have become an integral component of their persona, and in some cases this overlay may have metamorphosed into a full-blown psychological problem. At this juncture, intensive educational therapy and counseling or psychotherapy may be the only viable recourses for repairing the extensive self-concept damage that has occurred (see Appendix 2).

Appendix 2

Psychological Problems

Psychological problems refer to a pattern of behavior and attitudes that can be traced to an emotional trauma or series of traumas, a temperamental predisposition, a significant family dysfunction, or a combination of these factors. Because the symptoms of psychological overlay can overlap with the symptoms of a psychological problem, misdiagnosis and inadequate intervention may occur. The challenge of making an accurate diagnosis and developing an appropriate treatment plan is compounded when students are concurrently struggling with both psychological overlay and psychological problems. For example, a student may be emotionally defensive and anxious because she's seriously dyslexic *and* because she was also abused. Such a child will require both learning assistance and psychological therapy.

Whereas psychological overlay is usually triggered by negative school experiences or other non-school-related factors, psychological problems are usually triggered by a deeply imprinted emotional ordeal. A child who has witnessed a horrifying incident or who is enmeshed in a volatile, hostile, and dysfunctional family system that generates fear, anger, insecurity, shame, or guilt is clearly at risk psychologically. So, too, is the child who has been physically or emotionally abused or molested or who has experienced a major tragedy such as the loss of a parent or sibling.

Children may also have an inherited genetic predisposition to psychological problems such a bipolar disorder, obsessive-compulsive disorder, or schizophrenia. Whatever the causal factors, psychological problems can certainly induce and magnify learning difficulties and can generate anger, depression, phobias, insecurity, anxiety, resistance, irresponsibility, and diminished self-confidence.

Determining whether a student is wrestling with psychological overlay or with a psychological problem that is causing or exacerbating his learning problems can be extremely challenging. Is a child depressed and rebellious because he is doing poorly in school, or is he doing poorly in school because he is depressed and rebellious? Making this judgment call can be difficult even for a competent school counselor or school psychologist, and another mental health professional (i.e., a licensed clinical psychologist, social worker, or psychiatrist) may need to be consulted.

RED FLAG SYMPTOMS OF A POSSIBLE PSYCHOLOGICAL PROBLEM

Disorganized Thinking

- Lack of orientation (awareness of time, place, and people)
- Delusions (persecution, grandeur—"My teacher hates me!")
- Sensory distortions (auditory and/or visual hallucinations)

Maladaptive Behaviors

- Social withdrawal (seclusion, detachment, inability to form friendships)
- Excessive sensitivity
- Unwillingness to communicate
- Chronic tantrums
- Superstitious activity (rituals that must be performed before doing a task)
- Extreme mood changes
- Excessive fantasizing
- Phobic reactions (fear of people or germs)
- Fixations (excessive and exclusive interest in something)
- Suicidal tendencies or threats
- Chronic explosive anger or hostility
- Depression
- Excessive fearfulness
- Excessive anxiety
- Chronic manipulative behavior
- Chronic bullying
- Chronic lying
- Chronic stealing
- Chronic need to control others

Physical Dysfunctions

- Bed-wetting (in older children)
- Incontinence (in older children)
- Repeated stomachaches or headaches (also may be symptomatic of a physical problem)
- Chronic sleep disturbances
- Eating disorder (anorexia or bulimia)

REFERRAL AND INTERVENTION

Teachers who believe that students are manifesting symptoms of a possible psychological problem should consult with the school psychologist, school social worker, school counselor, or the appropriate school administrator. Accurate diagnosis of the underlying causal factors and effective treatment are vital antidotes to children's emotional distress, irrespective of whether this distress reflects psychological overlay or a psychological problem. The efficacy of these antidotes clearly hinges on timely intervention. The sooner a child's learning problems, psychological overlay, or psychological problems are competently identified and addressed, the less compelling the child's need to hang onto self-defeating conduct and the lower the risk of lasting psychological damage.

Index

NOTE: Page numbers in italics refer to figures.

**CORWIN
PRESS**

The Corwin Press logo—a raven striding across an open book—represents the union of
courage and learning. Corwin Press is committed to improving education for all learners by
publishing books and other professional development resources for those serving the field of
K–12 education. By providing practical, hands-on materials, Corwin Press continues to
carry out the promise of its motto: **"Helping Educators Do Their Work Better."**